Praise for CHASI...

MW00986882

*"Any person who has ever daydreamed about traveling the world to conquer her personal goals and passions will love Amy's chronicle. From the first chapter to the last page, I felt as if I was reliving my own past surf travels. A sense of freedom, overcoming fears, discovering new cultures, dealing with love, the exciting, unexplainable feeling of riding a wave—this is what Chasing Waves is all about.*

—Mary Osborne, pro surfer and co-author of
*Sister Surfer: A Woman's Guide to Surfing with Bliss and Courage*

*"Like a big, smooth wave peeling toward everybody who loves a good story, Chasing Waves takes you along on the surf-obsessed walkabout you've always dreamed of, but never had a chance to do. The people, the places, the loves, the losses, and the aching curiosity about one's own destiny and motivations—it's all rendered here in strong, fresh prose. This beautiful, worthy book has a place in every surf-literature home library, and is doubtless just the beginning of a great writer's career."*

—Daniel Duane, author of *Caught Inside:
A Surfer's Year on the California Coast*

*"With love and respect for the ocean, Chasing Waves captures the soul of surfing and the search for adventure from a female perspective."*

—Isabelle "Izzy" Tihanyi, founder and co-owner
of Surf Diva Surf School

*"Amy Waeschle has written a beautiful book that will make you laugh, make you cry, and make you go seek out a surfboard and the nearest ocean. Lyrical, heartfelt, and flat-out entertaining, this book is one wave that you must catch."*

—Jeff Shelby, author of *Wicked Break* and *Killer Swell*

*"I also have spent much of my life dreaming of bikinis, boards, and green waves; hence, I followed a very similar quest to Amy's—that of becoming an efficient and competent surfer. Her book left me in stitches! Enjoy it as an armchair adventure read, and marvel at how conquering our fears makes us stronger, more confident people in everyday life."*

—Alison Gannett, world champion extreme skier
and award-winning global cooling consultant

# CHASING WAVES

*A Surfer's Tale of*
*Obsessive Wandering*

## AMY WAESCHLE

THE MOUNTAINEERS BOOKS

**THE MOUNTAINEERS BOOKS**
*is the nonprofit publishing arm of The Mountaineers Club, an organization founded in 1906 and dedicated to the exploration, preservation, and enjoyment of outdoor and wilderness areas.*

1001 SW Klickitat Way, Suite 201, Seattle, WA 98134

Portions of this text previously appeared in altered form in the Patagonia catalog.

Certain surfing locations have been left vague or their names have been changed. This is intentional and is intended to preserve the sense of discovery shared by all surfers.

Manufactured in the United States of America

Copy Editor: Colin Chisholm
Cover Design: Karen Schober
Book Design and Layout: Mayumi Thompson
Cover photograph: © Caroline Woodham/Getty Images
Back cover photograph: *Amy Waeschle after surfing Namo Beach, Kadavu Island, Fiji* (Photo by Kurt Waeschle)

*Library of Congress Cataloging-in-Publication Data*
Waeschle, Amy.
  Chasing waves : a surfer's tale of obsessive wandering / Amy Waeschle.—1st ed.
    p. cm.
  ISBN 978-1-59485-113-1 (ppb)
  1. Waeschle, Amy. 2. Surfers—United States—Biography. 3. Surfing.
I. Title.
  GV838.W33 2009
  797.3'2092—dc22
  [B]
                  2009009467

# FOR KURT

"Listen: when someone tells me he or she wants to learn the
athleticism, the art, of surfing, my first reaction is invariably, 'Careful,
it can change everything.'"
—Alan Weisbecker, *In Search of Captain Zero*

"...the point being, I now know for certain, not the thrill of risk or
the pride of achievement, but rather the dailiness of well-spent time,
the accumulation of moments that will never translate into anything
but a private sense of well-being."
—Daniel Duane, *Caught Inside*

# CONTENTS

# PREFACE

I REMEMBER THE EXACT MOMENT I realized my love for surfing had become an obsession. I sat across from my husband on a remote beach in Washington State, my five-millimeter wetsuit peeled past my bikini top to my waist, the morning sun warming my shoulders. Late summer breezes stirred the leaves of the alders edging the shore, and the faint hiss and growl of the surf drifted over the dunes. Our morning session of playful waves had ended only because we craved coffee and the lineup had grown to more than ten surfers—crowded for those parts. It was the perfect summer moment. I should have been blissfully satisfied, but I wasn't.

I was frustrated by the lack of wave time available to us in the Northwest. Unlike in California or even Oregon, Washington's surfing beaches are far from metropolitan areas, accessible only after many hours of driving. Unless we decided to relocate to the fringes (think double-wides, red-checked flannel, and lots and lots of moss), live off the land (think fish, moonshine, and moss), surfing could be only an occasional pastime, a way to fill up free weekends when the conditions looked promising. Which was another thorn in my side: often we'd make the five-hour pilgrimage to the coast only to find the winds too strong, the swell direction not quite right, or because of missing the early ferry, we'd also missed the tide. So instead of surfing, we'd drive around, chasing our tails, knowing that we'd been skunked yet again.

I was hungry to be a better surfer, a good surfer—like Kurt and our surfing buddy Rick. I'd read about a place where I could make this happen. A place with warm water and perfect waves that peeled the length of endless beaches the color of cinnamon and gold. No camping in the cold rain. No wetsuits. No getting skunked. No moss.

"Let's go to Costa Rica," I blurted.

Kurt took another sip of his coffee and eyed me warily. "Er, yeah, someday."

"No," I replied. "In October."

Kurt looked alarmed. "This isn't about that surf camp again, is it?"

Kurt had learned to surf as a kid in Southern California. Back then nobody taught surfing; you just grabbed a board and paddled out and got thrashed. One day you figured out how to catch a wave, and in a few years you *might* actually figure out how to stand up on one. I was a twenty-nine-year-old woman. I didn't have that kind of time or patience. Plus, I'd grown up attending camps of all kinds: basketball, crew, Girl Scouts. Why not surfing?

"You just need time in the water," Kurt said, crossing his arms.

"Which isn't exactly happening here," I replied, narrowing my gaze. The surf camp I'd read about promised lessons twice a day in conditions of all kinds. I was sure that a week there would boost my skills and confidence.

"I can't get the time off work," Kurt said. "And besides, surf camps are for kooks."

I grimaced inwardly at the thought of being associated with a kook—a tactless, graceless idiot. "What if I go without you?"

Kurt looked at me in total disbelief. This was a break in our pact. Kurt isn't just my husband, he is my best friend. We do everything together: mountain biking, backpacking, skiing, and now surfing. How could I leave Kurt at home to bust his chops at work while I was halfway to the equator, sampling perfect surf? Maybe I was taking this surfing thing too far.

"Okay, okay." I looked away. "It was just an idea." Deep down, however, I wondered if I'd really let it go.

During the drive home that afternoon, I heard Kurt sigh. "This Costa Rica thing. If it's what you really want . . . "

"You mean you'll go?"

He shrugged, grudgingly. "But I'm not surfing alongside a bunch of kooks."

I grinned. "Deal."

Turns out there were a handful of kooks (just like anywhere), but Kurt handled it fine. The problem was me: I figured that once I was able to surf at an acceptable level, I could sit back and enjoy the pleasure of riding waves. No more sprinting to the coast at every opportunity. No more being frustrated and anxious when the conditions weren't right. Surely, Costa Rica and the skills I would obtain there would cure my surfing obsession.

I was wrong. It amplified it.

# 1

# WHY BOYFRIENDS MAKE
# TERRIBLE SURF INSTRUCTORS

I HAD NO INTENTION OF BEING A SURFER. After graduating from college with a geology degree and spending five years living intermittently out of my car to pursue the dirtbag lifestyle of a climbing and skiing bum, I saw myself as a mountain girl. My ultimate vacation fantasy was a three-week white-water canoe trip in the Brooks Range, or a backpacking traverse of outer Mongolia. I assumed surfing was something people did only in warm climates, in front of pretty, white-sand beaches. The ocean temperature in the Northwest hovered in the forties; the water was grayish green, and often stormy.

But shortly after starting my new life as a middle-school science teacher in a small island community in Washington State, I went to Mexico with my boyfriend, whom I had met on the Internet, a nice guy named Kurt who happened to be a surfer.

"Let's go surfing," he said one morning when, after three days of relaxing, sunbathing, and walking on the beach, we realized we were bored stiff. "I could teach you."

I was game. I remembered visiting my grandparents in Hawaii when I was six years old, and like every other kid I played around on a boogie board and discovered the joy of riding waves. I never forgot it.

The bus to Playa Linda sighed to a stop at the curb and we joined the queue of locals: men wearing drooping dungarees and thin sweaters; women in long dresses, their thick fingers adorned with chunky turquoise jewelry; a group of teenagers in nylon sweatsuits. I felt completely out of place wearing a t-shirt, board shorts, and flip-flops and bear-hugging a large foam slab that was now called a body board. Kurt looked cool and relaxed, a rented nine-foot-long surfboard tucked snugly under his arm. The longboard was for the surf lessons he had offered and the body board was for backup; if the waves were too big I would have something to do while he surfed.

Then the bus driver would not let us on the bus. He barked at us in Spanish, something to do with the longboard. Embarrassed, we heeded his wild gesticulations and hurried to the rear door. I got on first and located a seat nearby. I was thinking maybe the longboard would fit down the aisle. Kurt and I could take turns holding it.

"Uh, Amy?" Kurt said from the bottom step. I turned to see the tip of the longboard jammed into the ceiling, the tail still hanging out of the bus. Kurt was braced against the back of the stairs, thoroughly wedged.

I helped Kurt re-maneuver, but we couldn't get the longboard inside the bus. The tail rested on the bottom step, the body was angled forward—blocking the exit and access to several rows—its nose kissing the ceiling. Kurt and I were sweating and breathing hard. I looked around to a sea of silent faces. Should we abandon ship? Rent a car to get to the waves? Return when we could speak Spanish?

The bus doors closed. Kurt shrugged, his eyes wide and innocent. I moved back to my seat and the bus lurched forward.

---

The bus accelerated onto a freeway and I began to relax. The warm air blowing in the windows held a faint hint of spices and sweetness, like warmed honey. Many of the passengers were old women accompanied by small children. The grandmothers carried woven baskets in their laps or at their feet, and they wore their black hair in loose knots, exposing wrinkled, kind eyes. The children were still and quiet, and I was struck by the absence of Game Boys, iPods, or other such distractions. The children seemed on their best behavior, as if a day at the beach with grandma was a special treat.

When I turned again to check on Kurt, I noticed that the grandma sitting behind him looked worried. As we exited the freeway onto a narrow and curvy road, I began to see why. The door behind Kurt was inexplicably open, the tail of the board merely resting on the bottom step. With the bus tilting at each turn, Kurt's balance was faltering. I watched him grip the longboard with one arm and brace himself with the other, his body leaning forward or back to counter the bus's increasing sway. My mind flashed back to the rental shop, where we were forced to leave a thousand-dollar deposit. I was calculating how long I could survive on ramen noodles if the board were damaged when I heard a small shout.

Kurt was flying out of the bus.

Like a cobra striking its prey, the grandma behind him snatched the back of Kurt's surf trunks. The two of them seemed to hang there for an instant, Kurt's body half-in, half-out of the bus, black pavement and a blur of green foliage racing by; then gravity seemed to shift and Kurt was returned to his position inside the bus. Relief consumed me and I glared at the bus driver. A tiny grin had planted itself on his weathered cheeks.

Thanks to Grandma, who kept her hand at the ready at every turn, Kurt, I, and the longboard made it to Playa Linda in one piece.

———————+———————

"OK, get ready," Kurt said above the rumble of an approaching wave as I slithered onto the surfboard. The wave grew louder and adrenaline spurred me. "Paddle!"

I stroked toward the beach with all my might and when the wave behind me caught up, I was steamrolled in a wall of frothy water that forced its way into my nose, ears, mouth, and completely rearranged my bikini. I came up sputtering and half-naked. "What happened?" I asked, struggling to find the sandy bottom so I could stand. I tried to see Kurt but there was too much hair in my eyes.

"You missed it," he replied.

"Huh?" I wondered how I could "miss" a wave that I had been in front of. It was like hailing a taxi just before being flattened by it.

"Yeah," he replied, as if what he meant was obvious. "Let's try it again."

I waded out to where Kurt was standing chest-deep in the tepid ocean, all the while trying not to get blasted by incoming slugs of white water. He turned the board around for me so it was facing the beach, and I wiggled onto it. I was still trying to find the balance point so as to avoid flipping or rolling it when Kurt shouted, "Paddle, paddle, PADDLE!"

Now, I am not without experience in the paddling department: I once won the 50-meter freestyle (I was ten), I rowed crew for the Junior National Team *and* the varsity team in college, and I spent a month touring Alaska by sea kayak. I know a thing or two about paddling. But the surfboard was not cooperating: my arms flapped wildly, my legs rolled and flopped. It was like trying to commandeer a huge, slippery trout.

"What am I doing wrong?" I asked, still panting after my next paddle/swim/spin cycle. A wall of white water pulsed toward us. This time, Kurt grabbed the board and told me to duck. Beneath the wave the water was calm and peaceful and a dreamy, dusky blue. I tried to absorb the tranquility and be cradled by the forces at work instead of feeling abused by them, but when I surfaced, Kurt wiped his face and said, "You're not paddling hard enough."

"*What?*" I replied. Did I mention that I spent most of my college years heaving on a portside oar?

Another wave hit us and when I surfaced, Kurt said, "Here, I'll show you," and mounted the board.

The wave approached, Kurt started paddling. Then, in one motion, he was on his feet, gliding toward the shore with white water curling at his heels like a pack of fluffy, well-trained poodles.

"See?" he called out above the roaring surf.

See *what?* I thought.

And so it went. Kurt wheeled the board around. I hopped on. He yelled paddlepaddlePADDLE! I flopped around and spun my arms and either got worked by the wave or started zooming toward the beach so fast I forgot what I was supposed to do next, or I sped forward at an angle and fell off because I didn't know how to stop. All scenarios ended with me gasping, confused, and feeling increasingly frustrated. I began to understand that boyfriends who teach themselves to surf at the tender age of seven by thrashing around and nearly drowning may not make the best surf instructors.

How was this supposed to be fun?

"Wait," I said as he was spinning the board around for the umpteenth time. "What comes after paddling?"

"The pop-up."

I frowned.

"It's when you stand up."

"How do you do that?"

He thought for a second then scowled. "I dunno. You just stand up."

I asked if I could try it on my own, and I thought Kurt looked relieved. I tried to paddle into a wave, I tried to pop up but it was no use. Half the time I couldn't even get the board turned around before a seething wall of white water swept me up and churned me like a rag doll. At one point I looked to the beach, hoping for some pointers but noticed that Kurt had fallen asleep beneath his sombrero.

I began to wonder if I should drop the whole surfing thing. Kurt was a nice guy, a firefighter who was sweet and funny and who liked to cook. My mother liked him, my friends liked him. I was beginning to really like him, too, and I sensed that he felt the same about me. This surfing lesson was the first time things hadn't been easy between us. Where was I going to surf anyway, except on once-a-year vacations like this one? The ocean was cold and scary in Washington State. Surely nobody surfed there.

"Maybe we can try a different beach," he suggested halfheartedly after I came in and sat beside him. My arms were so tired that I was dragging the surfboard. I felt like I had ingested so much seawater that I would have the runs for a week.

"Sure," I replied, equally halfheartedly. I eyed the cluster of surfers out beyond the shorebreak, occasionally dropping into shimmering blue walls of water. I nodded in their general direction. "Why don't you go surf?"

"Nah," he replied, sounding tired as he traced circles in the sand with a stick. "We should probably head back."

Then I felt bad. After coming all this way, after surviving a death-defying bus ride, protecting the longboard and my savings, after failing to impart his surfing knowledge, however meager, he was too worn out to enjoy himself.

I decided that maybe surfing wasn't something I was supposed to do in this life.

But before following Kurt, I watched another surfer glide into a wave, its silky blue surface glistening in the sun; the surfer a black figure, dancing. Maybe I was giving up too quickly.

Maybe there was another way to become a surfer.

Maybe.

# 2

## FEET LIKE BLOCKS OF ICE, HEART RED-HOT WITH JOY

STANDING ON THE FROZEN SHORE of Tofino's Chesterman Beach, I realized with sudden panic that I must be out of my mind. The ocean looked chilly enough for icebergs and was likely home to great white sharks and deathly currents that could whisk me halfway to Siberia. My only protection would be five millimeters of neoprene and a nine-foot foam surfboard with a smooth plastic underside and a surface resembling the rubbery nonslip mat in the bottom of my grandma's bathtub.

When I had signed up with Surf Sister, an all-women's surf school on the west coast of Vancouver Island in the woodsy and very wet town of Tofino, January seemed like a fine time for surf lessons—after Christmas break my teaching schedule wasn't yet crazy, we'd beat the crowds, and lodging was cheap.

Clearly, I had not thought this through: subarctic, coastal Canada + January = frigid temperatures, frigid ocean = frigid, popsicled Amy. But Karen, my blonde and chipper instructor who lived in that freezing wilderness, assured me that the cold would be the least of our worries. "Then what will we worry about," I asked, "getting mauled by sharks?" Karen just laughed.

———————+———————

"Goofy-foot or regular?" Karen asked after we had hiked to the beach and laid our longboards facedown in the sand.

Because I had tried snowboarding, I had the answer. "Regular," I replied, which meant that I stood with my left foot forward. This meant that on waves breaking right (as in from right to left, looking at the horizon) I would surf toe-side, or facing the wave. On left-breaking waves I would forever ride backside.

Karen drew outlines of our longboards in the cold gray sand with her fingers and for the next hour I was her dryland protégé, paddling my sand surfboard in time with imaginary incoming waves. We talked about safety and how to cover our heads in a wipeout and how to hold onto our boards in the white water. We practiced the art of the pop-up. When Karen proclaimed me ready for the waves, my knees started knocking. Or was it just the cold?

We stood at the edge of the water, the sound of the surf a constant, droning rumble. Forget thoughts of tranquility and peace; I was freaked out of my mind. Rolling lines of swell extended from the horizon, marching toward shore like Higgins boats on D-day. They crested into towering walls before exploding into big piles of white water that swished up the beach, leaving mounds of foam and flotsam. How would I keep from drowning?

I followed Karen's example and pulled the hood of my wetsuit over my head, trying in vain to tuck in my hair with heavily gloved fingers, then made sure my wetsuit bootie straps were fastened as tight as possible around my ankles. The beach was a wide-open park, with people walking, playing Frisbee with their dogs, riding bikes, scuttering around the tide pools. The air temperature hovered in the forties and the sky was a mottled gray, layered with ashen clouds. The previous night's heavy rain that had pelted the roof of the cozy cabin where Kurt and I were staying had left a silvery sheen on the huge, ancient trees guarding the edge of the beach.

"You'll feel a rush of cold water getting into your suit," Karen said as we started wading. "Don't panic, it's normal."

Sure enough, the icy ocean greeted me by seeping into the vacant spaces of my wetsuit; first down past my toes, then up behind my knees, and finally, as I jumped over an incoming wave, down my neck, arms, and chest. This was *normal*? I shivered uncontrollably. How would I last two hours? I tried to look on the bright side—this being so close to the Arctic, the local paramedics were probably crackerjacks when it came to thawing frozen surfers.

Standing next to me in belly-deep water, Karen turned my enormous board around to face the shore. At her command I flopped onto it and tried to keep from rolling off. I remembered Mexico and my failed lesson. Was I nuts for thinking Canada and Karen were going to be any better?

I was still squirming on the board when I heard an approaching wave. An electric shock of terror zipped through me (wasn't I about to get creamed?) when Karen said, "Paddle!"

I thrashed forward, digging in the way Karen had instructed on the beach. I felt Karen give my board a little push, then the wave picked me up and I was soaring forward. I had it! I heeded Karen's advice and paddled three more times to be sure I *really* had it, then lurched to my feet. I was surprised to find myself standing. I had just caught a wave! Delight sprouted from my frigid toes to my hooded head and for that instant, my anxiety was forgotten. But just as quickly, the board wobbled and I fell face-first into the knee-deep water.

I struggled to stand and heard Karen's hooting. She was clapping her gloved hands above her head and her smile was like sunshine. I paddled into another wave and found I could stand a little longer. Each time I learned more about how to stay balanced and how to position my body. Over and over we repeated this exercise, and despite my leaden arms and frozen feet, by the time Karen and I called it quits, I was hooked.

Doubt returned when Karen told me that tomorrow's session would take place beyond the shorebreak, a place she called "the lineup," where the waves were still silky and unbroken and where surfers waited to catch them. I put the pieces together and imagined myself far from shore, dangling my feet over bloodthirsty sharks. Standing up if I wanted to rest, or jumping over incoming waves would not be possible. Goosebumps sprouted even though my wetsuit was toasty warm after paddling nonstop for two hours. "Are you sure I'm ready for that?" I asked.

Karen just grinned and arched an eyebrow. "See you tomorrow."

Back at the car I huffed and puffed for fifteen minutes to get out of my wetsuit, which had adhered to me like shrink wrap. Once cozy in dry clothes and a wool hat, however, I felt a warm, energizing glow—a sensation I would enjoy many times to come. When I saw Kurt on the beach, walking toward me wearing a huge grin, I saw that he was feeling it, too.

"That was so awesome," he said with quivering, blue lips—he's one of those tall and lean types whose furnace seems to be set a few ticks lower than the rest of the well-padded world's. His eyes were the same color as the slate-blue ocean and his black eyelashes glistened with seawater. We walked back to the car together.

"I mean, I'm freezing my ass off but the waves were amazing and it's beautiful. Plus there's nobody in the water."

Like me, Kurt had never considered Washington or Canada surfing destinations, and like me he was wrong. After our failed lesson in Mexico, I had told him that I still wanted to learn. He was dubious, confessing that when he left California he had been ready to give up surfing altogether because of the crowds and attitude. But then we discovered Surf Sister and decided to give Tofino a try.

"I'm so glad we did this," he said after loading the boards. He gave me a kiss, his freckled cheeks cold and wet.

I described my lesson to him while he changed out of his wetsuit. I was keyed up with the possibilities flashing before my eyes: here's Kurt and Amy, trading waves in Waikiki; here's Kurt and Amy, charging huge surf in Bali; here's Kurt and Amy, having a sunset session in Costa Rica.

That night, after an excellent meal of local seafood and a spicy Chilean red wine, I lay in bed, listening to the surf. Did it sound bigger than the night before? I was frightened enough to seriously question the safety of our cabin—located a good hundred meters uphill from the ocean. In reality, only a tsunami would have been a threat, but still I tossed and turned, dreading the next day.

I woke early and tried to calm my nerves with a hot shower. It didn't work and I spent the remaining half hour before my lesson fighting cramping bowels and sprinting to the toilet. Kurt tried to tell me that in the dark, waves always sound bigger and that if Karen didn't think it was safe, she wouldn't let me paddle out. I tried to see myself paddling past the thick lines of pounding surf. How would I make it through the heaving shorebreak to the outside?

Because it was so cold, Kurt and I drove to the beach in our still damp but at least warm wetsuits, something so taboo in California, he told me, that we would be laughed out of town. "But this is survival!" he said with chattering teeth as we pulled up to the woodsy parking strip.

The huge pines dripped with the previous night's rain and smelled of sap and loamy earth. We walked through them in silence to the broad, sandy beach, which was shrouded in a band of wispy mist. The clear sky above glowed a pale, icy blue. It would have been stunning if I hadn't been so focused on the pounding surf. How big were the waves? Three feet? Ten? I took deep, slow breaths to calm my insides, but it didn't work. I was about to duck into the woods when I saw Karen approaching from the ocean, carrying her longboard beneath her arm and smiling. It put me at ease knowing she had surfed that morning's waves unscathed. Kurt gave me a quick kiss before heading south for the peak he'd surfed the day before. "Have fun," he said with a grin.

Karen and I reviewed the previous day's paddling and pop-up sequences before she added another skill that captured my attention: the turtle roll. It's a safety measure in which surfer and surfboard can slip underneath a breaking wave in deep water. Karen modeled gripping the side-rails of the board, flipping it over (so as to be suspended beneath it) while the imaginary wave broke above. Supposedly I wouldn't be thrashed in the process and could flip over and resume paddling out. I was unconvinced.

"*Never* ditch your board," Karen warned with a look that could melt steel. "It's dangerous. For you, for other surfers. Plus, everybody will think you're a kook."

"What's a kook?" I asked.

Karen clucked her tongue. "Someone who can't surf."

"But I can't surf."

Karen paused, her eyes narrowing. "A kook doesn't know what they're doing. A kook puts their wetsuit on backward or talks too much in the lineup." She lifted an eyebrow. "Get it?"

I vowed never to do anything that would make me look like a kook.

We waded into the icy surf, jumping over a few waves until there was a lull, and then Karen told me to paddle like hell. I felt a pang of dread as I mounted my board and paddled forward with deep, hard strokes. But my arms, tired from yesterday's paddling, felt like they were made of wood and Karen steadily pulled away from me.

My breath came in shaky gusts, my eyes fixed on the horizon, messy with cresting and crashing waves. I paddled over turbulent piles of white water without falling off my board and thought, *this isn't so hard* . . . until I saw a thick wedge of a wave rising up in front of me. My fingers tingled, my heaving breath became ragged. I had an overwhelming urge to let go of my board and swim beneath the wave like I had in Mexico, but I remembered Karen's hard look and my arms tore through the water. The wave loomed. I watched the lip begin to feather. *Oh my God I am going to get creamed!* I thought. Karen's "Never ditch your board" rang in my ears as my fingers tightened around the rails and I rolled over, squinting my eyes shut and holding my breath. My feet flailed and water rushed up my nose. I felt a small tug upward that helped me flip myself back over; when I surfaced I was gasping for breath and still thrashing.

But I was okay. The wave had left me behind.

My momentary relief was quickly replaced by another rush of fear—the next wave was upon me. My heart raced as I stroked hard for the outside, my arms burning. Somehow I soared over the crest just in time and the folding wave receded behind me. Several more waves stood in my path before I could clear the impact zone, so I dug deep and paddled with everything I had. By the time I reached Karen, I was exhausted to the point of tears and had so much hair in my face I must have looked like Chewbacca from *Star Wars*.

"You made it," Karen said, beaming. "Nice." She sat calmly on her board, facing the wintry horizon.

I copied Karen's posture, wiggling a little as I figured out my balance and caught my breath. Waves broke in distinct peaks along the beach, with clusters of surfers sitting together at each, one by one dropping into waves. I was thankful that Karen and I were alone at ours. I was so tired and frazzled that I wasn't sure I had the guts to compete with anyone.

Slowly my anxieties and exhaustion eased. Being outside, where waves were non-threatening lines of unbroken swell, the currents not zipping me to Siberia, I realized that Karen had been right; I wasn't worried about the cold, or sharks for that matter.

And in that moment, actually, I wasn't worried about much of anything; it was peaceful out there. The breaking surf was a distant shushing and the rhythmic pulsing of waves was soothing, not terrorizing. Birds soared across the ocean's surface, visiting the tiny rock islands beyond or occasionally dive-bombing for fish. The water was so clear I could see past my dangling feet to fat ridges of peppery sand. The air was crisp and clean and sunlight heated my cheeks. I took a deep breath and drank in the moment, wondering if it was possible to feel what I thought I felt.

I belonged there.

"OK, get ready!" Karen said, yanking me from my reverie.

I spun my board around, got prone, and started paddling. My skin prickled with fear. The wave began to fold and I heard Karen's, "Go, go, go!"

The wave bobbed me upward and I dug in three more times, certain that I was about to be swept up like a lawn chair in a hurricane, but nothing happened. I looked on, confused, as the wave continued without me.

I was surprised that instead of relief, I felt disappointed.

"It happens a lot when you're learning," Karen explained when I returned to her side.

I remembered Mexico and gritted my teeth. "Am I not paddling hard enough?"

Karen shook her head. "Your paddling is fine. It's your timing."

"How do I learn that?"

Karen smiled. "Practice." She must have seen the apprehension in my eyes because she added, "Don't worry, we'll get you a wave!" Something on the horizon caught her eye, and I followed her gaze to a steely blue ridge of swell steadily approaching. "Get ready!" Karen said.

Again I paddled when she told me and dug in when I thought I had the wave, but it lumbered on without me. Disheartened, I returned to Karen's side. Our session would be coming to an end soon. If I didn't figure out how to ride a wave then, who would teach me?

Karen suggested we move in toward the shore just a little. This time I spotted the wave and Karen smiled. "This is it," she said, her eyes twinkling. I spun around and started paddling, asking my muscles for every last ounce of speed. Karen's encouraging words echoed through my mind as I felt the wave's surge. I gave it three more strokes and noticed that I was still gliding. I had it! I stood up.

Euphoria filled me. I was surfing! The board glided down the crest and the wave broke behind me, sending me straight toward the beach at what felt like Mach 10. When the wave died out, I hopped off and looked back at Karen who was wahooing with joy as she raised her arms in victory.

Later, after offering big thanks to Karen, I met up with Kurt and we paddled out together. By then we were both tired and cold, but sitting in the lineup together beneath a hazy winter sun, listening to the birds and the swish of pounding surf, I felt as if a key had slid neatly into a lock, opening a door that revealed a whole new world. I paddled for a few waves, missing most of them but catching one or two and reveling in Kurt's praise. He of course outshined me by catching all the waves he paddled for, surfing "down the line" of the wave, or parallel to it, even adding in a turn or two, but I didn't care. I now understood the basics. I hoped that I would progress quickly and, with practice, be able to catch more and more waves and ride them like a real surfer— along the green face instead of straight for the beach. I wondered if reaching that point would make my fear subside.

"Can we come back?" I asked Kurt as we plodded toward the car, our muscles tired but our spirits high.

"Definitely," he replied.

I took one last glance at the broad scoop of coastline, with the soft sand and towering, ancient trees. I felt like I was on the brink of a grand journey.

If only I had known just how far it would take me.

# 3

# SURF LESSONS FROM CAPTAIN ALOHA

"PATT-ULL HARD, EMMIE!" The dreadlocked man shouted as I paddled forward, gritting my teeth with determination. "Patt-ull!"

The hissing wave rose up behind me, sucking up gallons of ocean water with it, growing larger, thicker, ever more destructive. I had the sudden image of myself marooned on dry reef with every drop of ocean poised to smash me to smithereens.

I glanced back to see the lip feathering, reaching outward, and at the same moment I heard "Not so hard, now, Emmieee!" from my newfound instructor, the trailing *eeee* cut off by the breaking wave cracking me on the head.

Once again, I was too late.

The wave plunged me into a tumultuous darkness that forced water into my sinuses and liberated my bikini. I came up sputtering and trying to preserve some form of modesty. I wiped the stinging salt from my eyes and began paddling the rented longboard that the shop owner told me would be fine for my purposes. As if. With all the time I had spent underwater, I should have asked for one equipped with a snorkel.

I made it past the pulses of white water to the lines of unbroken swell outside and steered toward the takeoff. Captain Aloha paddled alongside me as I neared the pack of other surfers.

"You kent patt-ul so hard you beat da wave," he said with a chuckle, his smile brighter than anything I might expect from a wrinkled face with no front teeth. I groaned inwardly, my frustration nearing the boiling point. Paddle hard or not so hard? Drop in, *then* turn along the wave, or steer into it at an angle? Wait for waves here or over there? Since my lesson with Karen, I had been practicing turning into waves instead of going straight, but it was tricky. Waves break left or right, and it is the surfer's challenge to line up at the point where that wave starts to break in one of those directions. So far, in attempting to ride a wave down the line, I had done a lot more paddling, missing waves, and getting worked than surfing.

Captain Aloha paddled off to the right and I watched his biceps ripple. He was probably not even breathing hard. His skin was as dark as molasses and his soft brown eyes were pure Hawaiian. He had appeared about an hour earlier, seemingly out of the waxing and waning mist. I had watched him talk with the local surfers in the lineup, so I knew he was one of them, and I had seen him surf with an enviable, effortless grace that I felt certain was the result of a lifetime passion.

People had warned me about surfing in the Aloha State, me being a *haole*, a white person, especially a non-Hawaiian. Supposedly the locals could be fiercely protective of their waves. But I felt none of that. In fact, this Captain Aloha—with his wild enthusiasm and his long, lumpy dreadlocks—had not seemed to notice that I was an outsider. Not only had he been friendly, he had started giving me pointers.

And I needed them. Despite my lesson with Surf Sister, becoming a skilled surfer continued to elude me. It was a little like skiing: after one lesson you can put on your skis, get on and off the chairlift, and power-wedge your way down the bunny slope.

After that, the gear gets more complicated, the lifts get faster, and the runs get steeper. A lot steeper.

But at least with skiing, you won't drown.

Or flash half the beach.

Originally, this trip to Kauai had not been planned as a surf vacation. I had stumbled across a cheap package deal and jumped at the chance for a break from the Northwest's gray, cold drizzle and the drama that comes with supervising 137 middle-schoolers—think hundreds of test tubes, carefully graded lab reports that kids don't read, and surging adolescent hormones packed into a lab area the size of your kitchen. The image of myself sitting on a beach, reading books, and drinking mai tais pulled at me like a tractor beam. I would just relax, take it easy. A low-key vacation.

Right.

I was quickly learning something about myself: I was not a sit-on-the-beach kind of gal.

So Kurt and I drove north to Hanalei, where dense, steamy rainforest rose to verdant heights and pine trees edged a crescent-shaped beach. The waves were tiny by Hawaiian standards but perfect for a newbie like me. The water transitioned from gin-clear to dusky turquoise depending on the sky's ever-changing mix of sun, rain, and clouds. I had seen sea turtles, polka-dotted fish, and, on the horizon, more than a half-dozen whale spouts. I had heard soft guitar music drifting from the shadows and seen barbeque smoke twisting upward through the pines. I watched a tattooed and burly man paddle out alongside his delicate-limbed little girl and a group of men launch and paddle an outrigger canoe through the surf and disappear around the point, their strokes practiced and sure. Wanting to be a part of that life—one so tied to the ocean—seemed as natural as putting one foot in front of the other.

But all I had managed to do was nosedive into the reef. Fortunately, the reef below me that day was fairly innocuous, not in shallow water or even very sharp. But the thought of getting cut up, like the guy I had seen in the parking lot that morning—his legs and one shoulder lined with pulpy red scratches—horrified me. Every time I wiped out I panicked, flailing wildly to keep my feet, hips, and hands close to the surface.

I'm sure I looked ridiculous—like the kook Karen warned me not to be. It was disheartening and frustrating as hell. I tried everything: repositioning myself on my board, adjusting my timing, standing up earlier, sitting farther outside or more toward shore. Even watching others didn't help—there were kids out there who were killing it—gliding into waves, arcing smooth turns, kicking out at the end with such grace and smooth panache it made me want to hide. That's when Captain Aloha appeared, playing with the waves as if he'd conjured them out of the depths himself. Maybe it was his pure happiness—as if he were the true spirit of Aloha—or just that he seemed so confident in me, but I put my faith in him.

His latest advice had me turning as I caught the wave. The reefy waves were steeper than I was used to, which may have been the reason why I kept nosediving, or "pearling," straight for the depths in the moment when I should have already been on my feet. Back home, my gently sloped beach breaks gave me all the time in the world to stand up, go straight, and then think about turning down the line. In Hanalei, it was all over in the blink of an eye.

I paddled to a less consistent but empty spot so that I could flail without the added pressure of being observed. I let several waves pass. I was tired and worn down. Would I ever get it?

A nicely forming wave approached and I found myself pivoting the nine-foot board around. Over my shoulder, I kept an eye on the wave, which was a kaleidoscope of turquoise, frosty blue, and pearly white that grew more transparent the more it rose up, revealing outlines of the stubby reef below. I tried to visualize turning the board as I dropped in and paddled a little to my right as the wave's hiss grew louder. This time I stroked in at an angle and it worked! For an instant I was facing the wall of water. Before I could enjoy it, however, I fell backward and was engulfed in swirling turbulence. I fought through stinging bubbles to the surface and yanked my leash to pull my board to me so I could slither onto it and paddle outside before the next wave came. I huffed and puffed. What had I done wrong now?

My smiling Captain Aloha caught my eye and shouted over the wave tops, as if reading my mind. "Yes! But when you stend up you cannot stend so straight. You fall over, eh?" He laughed and his eyes twinkled. I squinted at him. "Bend da knees, eh?" added my coach, patting his own for emphasis. In one smooth motion Captain Aloha spun, lowered onto his board, and with exactly three easy strokes he stood, turned toe-side, and rode the peeling wave all the way to the beach. I couldn't help but feel a twinge of despair when he stepped onto the pale sand with his board tucked under his arm. He was leaving me? *Now?*

I sat quietly and gazed out to a cluster of dark specks that were surfers, Kurt among them somewhere, picking off waves that formed with machinelike regularity. The water shimmered in the sun, each wave crest exploding with white spray as it folded, chasing its rider. I wondered if I would ever be good enough to surf waves like that. Kurt and I had tied the knot a few months earlier and were planning a late honeymoon trip to Fiji—the land of perilous reefs. How would I manage to surf there if I couldn't even manage the harmless reef below my dangling feet?

I decided that with my dwindling spirit and my guru gone, I should take my last wave in. Once I was home, I reasoned, I would work on my timing, my form, and my wave selection. I would try to remember Captain Aloha's words.

My wave came and while paddling with leaden arms, I heard Captain Aloha's encouraging "Patt-ull, Emmie!" from the beach. My enthusiasm returned. The wave rose behind me as I angled into it, and I heard "Stend Up! Stend up, Emmie!" I hopped to my feet, knees bent this time. I landed a little late but managed to recover and soon I was soaring, the turquoise water sheeting out in front of me. For the first time that day the adrenaline in my veins wasn't born of fear, but jubilation. I rode the wave until my fin hit the sand, then looked toward my surf guru, whose toothless smile I returned with bubbling laughter. I felt like jumping up and down or doing some kind of wiggly dance.

Forget *that* being my last wave. I found a sudden rush of energy and paddled back out, my arms somehow weightless. I wanted more. The magic was still there and soon I was lost in the moment, catching wave upon wave, sailing down the line, the energy from Mother Ocean filling my soul.

When it was time to go, I removed my leash and wrapped it around the tail of my board while contentedly curling my toes into the sun-warmed sand. I squinted at the glittering bay to find my surf guru. I wouldn't have been surprised if he'd vanished, a figment of my imagination or some kind of spirit. But I spotted him a ways down the beach alongside a new protégée, laughing, gesticulating wildly with his hands. Satisfied, I turned away, surfboard snug at my side and the genuine meaning of Aloha understood.

# 4

## OVER MY HEAD IN FIJI

I ATTACHED THE THICK VELCRO LEASH to my ankle and looked once more at our boat driver, a thick-trunked Fijian with a wiry helmet of black hair and wide, deeply creased feet. He offered me a curious smile, probably wondering what a woman was doing out there—shouldn't I be home, pounding taro root and drying fish alongside the other wives?

All the terror I had ever felt before that moment seemed so trivial I could have laughed, but all I could utter was a meek, high-pitched peep. Surely I was about to die.

A distant wave exploded, sending a spray of fine mist into the bright blue sky and emitting a deep, thunderous roar. I breathed deeply but it had no effect on my pounding heart.

I climbed over the gunnels and slipped into the ocean, which felt like bathwater and looked like all the pictures you've ever seen of tropical seas: clear water over a calico pattern of pale or dark patches depending on what's underneath—powdery white sand, chunky reef, or open, deep water. Another wave rumbled. I was trembling.

Fiji's reef-generated waves break so far from shore that getting on a boat is the only way to reach them. Reefs fringe many

of Fiji's islands, but only a handful have the proper setup for surfing because of what's called a "keyhole," a break in the reef that
creates a deep-water channel. Swell hits the reef and peels along
it, breaking in a smooth line like dominoes falling, then dies out
in the channel. The channel offers boats a protected anchorage
and access to the open seas beyond; for surfers, the channel is the
safe house, the on-ramp, and the end zone. At that moment I was
grateful for the deep-water safe haven, as it allowed me to size up
the waves without having to put myself in their jaws.

Unfortunately, that did nothing to dampen my certainty of a
serious ass-kicking. Each wave seemed bigger than the last, towering above the reef like a great serpent rearing up to strike. I saw
myself cartwheeling down the face, the weight of half an ocean
about to detonate on my head; I would certainly meet the reef,
which is very much alive in those parts. Alive and very, very sharp.
I'd be cut to ribbons, for sure.

The wave in my sights that day was called Resorts due to its
close proximity to where Kurt and I had booked a ten-day stay,
and also because it is the least powerful of the half-dozen in the
area, making it the experienced surfer's pick for *least* desirable
(earning it the nickname *Last* Resorts). That someone could think
this wave not powerful amazed me. Nothing separated that reef
from the storms of the southern Arctic. Those waves carried the
strength to sink oil tankers.

Kurt was ahead of me, exiting the deep channel and steering
left, toward the takeoff. The fat ridges of swell were so massive that
their troughs swallowed him. It was starting to make me seasick,
as I, too, approached the open sea. The waves' steady growls had
become mixed with the firecracker sizzle of mist being sheared
from their backs by an offshore wind. As I turned away from the
channel and entered the lion's den, this mist raked my cheeks like
ice crystals.

Suddenly I noticed that the approaching wall was big enough to break on me. My ears throbbed with the sudden release of adrenaline as I aimed toward the wave and stroked hard for the outside. If that wave broke on me I would be swept over the reef, caught inside, and probably drowned. The wave approached, its turquoise lip thinning and fraying into vapor. I paddled up, up the steep wall. The sound of my panicked breathing was replaced by the ominous hiss of the wave, looming like a hatchet. I saw the white tip of my board against the sky and then I was catapulted over the lip. Beneath me, the intense, hungry power of the wave tugged me backward but I scratched and dug. Somehow I managed to pull away. I heard the shuddering *boom* and was blasted by shards of mist. I yearned to lie there and recover but was forced onward to avoid the next wave, and the next.

Forget surfing. This was survival. By the time I reached the relative safety of the outside, I was completely drained.

I blamed the glossy brochures; they had seduced me with images of white-sand beaches and surfers catching pretty waves. But there was nothing pretty about my predicament. Fiji felt hostile and wicked. And there were no beaches anywhere near our resort. The ring of barrier reef not only trapped the swell, it seemed to have trapped the sand, too. The shoreline in front of our resort consisted of sticky, brown mud. Reaching the skiff that delivered us to Resorts required a knee-deep wade though a murky lagoon, my feet sinking into gushy sediment that ate one of my flip-flops. When the tide was out, the bay looked like a mud flat and reeked of rotting fish.

Kurt sat facing the ocean and didn't see me approach. When he pivoted and began paddling for a wave, I had the urge to shout, "No!" He dropped in and the wave quickly folded, obliterating him from sight. The wave had eaten him alive.

I sat up on my board and craned my neck to watch Kurt's

wave in the hope of catching a glimpse of him. An eternity passed before I saw him fly over the lip, which punched shut behind him in a cloud of white spray. As he paddled closer, I was shocked to see him grinning.

"It's way more mellow than it looks," he told me with bright eyes.

Another wave exploded nearby. "Yeah, right," I said, keeping one eye on the horizon for sneaker sets.

"Really," he insisted. "It's super forgiving."

Before I could protest further, he pivoted and disappeared behind another wave.

A monster set approached and I paddled furiously over it, away from the takeoff. I decided to move down the reef a bit. Maybe I'd be less scared if I could paddle into a wave later, after it had broken and was a little bit smaller. After what felt like two minutes but was probably more like half an hour, I finally got up my nerve and decided to take a wave. I'd paid a lot of money and endured epic travel conditions to get there. I tried to think positive.

*I can do this.*

My heart told me otherwise the minute I began paddling— ramming so hard against my chest that I wondered if it was trying to break free. I imagined it crying out to the other organs, "Get out now! Save yourselves!" I paddled forward and the wave scooped me up. Suddenly I was looking down, down, down the steepest drop of my life. Every fiber of my being resisted and I pulled up. The wave surged ahead and exploded, its cold, gravely mist blowing into my face. Gasping for breath, I turned around and paddled far into the horizon. I *didn't* think I could do it, eighty bucks a day and seventeen hours of hellish travel or not.

Fiji is a country with clean, neatly dressed schoolchildren and untrammeled rain forest but horrible roads and surprisingly bland food (I had never eaten so much chicken). Most surfers associate Fiji with Tavarua, a tiny speck of land off the main island of Viti

Levu and the resort with the exclusive surfing rights to world-class Cloudbreak, a barreling, freight-train left. Fijians don't surf. Many of them can't even swim. I scanned the horizon and couldn't say I blamed them. Where would they swim to? Japan?

Kurt paddled up to me. "You okay?"

I didn't know what to say, so I said nothing.

"It's not that bad," he said.

I'm sure he saw my disbelief when our eyes met. I wondered if he could also see the disappointment I felt in myself.

"Come on," he said. "You gotta try it."

"What if I get caught inside?"

"You won't."

"What if I fall?"

He shrugged. "It's pretty deep. I haven't hit the reef once. You'll be fine."

I sighed.

"Come on," he said with an encouraging smile.

Reluctantly I followed him to the lineup. We sat upright on our boards, scanning the horizon. Kurt was silent and I was glad for this, as the voices in my head were so loud I couldn't have carried on a conversation or listened to advice. Besides, Kurt is good that way; he knows my limits and has not once patronized me. I realized that he would never encourage me to surf this wave if he didn't think I was capable.

Maybe I *could* do it.

A smooth, fat ridge of a wave rose out of the deep and I decided to claim it. I spun around but waited to paddle until the wave got closer. Over my shoulder, I kept an eye on the crest, which was building, its thinning lip glowing like stained glass. In a burst of speed, I paddled forward. My heart leapt into my throat as once again I stared down, down, down into the deep blue trough. I took one last stroke to steer left then sprang to my feet. Suddenly, I was moving so fast I wondered if I was flying.

Elation filled me. I sensed the wave crumbling, its jet-engine roar crowding my ears and the force of it pushing against my back. I was aware but didn't dare look at the lip curling high above me; my eyes were glued to the soft slope of the shoulder, to where I could carve a direct line and exit over the lip.

But I fell before I could get there.

The back of my head slammed against the water and my feet were flipped over my head. The wave engulfed me. I was in a thundercloud of water, with bubbles stinging my skin and currents ripping at my limbs. The leash of my surfboard tugged hard at my ankle—what if it broke? If I lost my board, I would be one small swimmer against this big, big sea. Panicked, I thrashed toward the surface, trying not to kick and therefore make contact with the reef. My arms clawed for purchase. I could only hope I was heading up. Someone back home told me that without the thick wetsuit I was used to wearing, I would lose a significant amount of buoyancy. I wondered just how true that was. How far was I from the surface—six inches? Six feet? My lungs burned. Finally I broke through and opened my mouth to sweet, sweet air. But incoming waves loomed, and I had to move.

I reeled in my board and paddled it furiously. I dug deep, calling on all my reserves. My breathing became focused. I concentrated on my strokes—I could not waste a single ounce of energy. I could not get caught inside. I begged the incoming wave to wait. Up the face I paddled, my eyes fixed on the place where frothy crest met sky. Spray crackled all around me and peppered my face. I closed my eyes.

My board launched over the wave and slammed down on the other side. The wave punched shut behind me with a booming roar. I melted with relief. But again, I could not stop. I fought my way over half a dozen waves in that way before reaching safety.

Finally, I rejoined Kurt. I wanted to curl up on my board and take a nice, long rest.

"How'd it go?" he asked.

Despite the terror, the awful experience inside that wave, the euphoria of riding it was the only thing that came to mind.

"Did you drop in?"

The memory of those few precious seconds would be with me for a long time. I nodded. "But then I fell."

He raised his eyebrows. "I wondered what happened to you. You okay?"

"Uh huh." A rush of seawater gushed from my nose and I nearly gagged.

"Got worked, huh?"

I nodded.

I paddled for a few more waves but always pulled up at the last minute. I saw that long drop and I remembered the full-tilt panic of being trapped underwater. I wasn't even sure why I was still out there.

"We should get going," Kurt said after returning from his umpteenth wave. "Tide's getting low."

I squinted back toward the boat and saw that our driver was standing, gazing in our direction as if to will us in. Earlier, he must have been sacked out because there had been no sign of him.

"One more?" I asked even though I wasn't confident it would happen.

"Sure," Kurt said. "See you in the channel," he added with a grin. And then he was off, the sizzle and boom of his wave erupting after him.

The wave I chose was lumpy and smallish. The wind had shifted from offshore—the most desirable of winds because it holds the faces up—to side-shore so I was blinded by spray when I dropped in. Somehow, when I popped up I landed ungloriously on my knees. It was a perplexing position to find myself in and one that rendered me powerless. Unpiloted, my board carved a smooth arc straight into the trough, where I was sheared from it to head-plant into the depths. My fight back to the outside took longer this time because I didn't make it over the incoming waves after I surfaced. I got to the crest—paddling hard but with arms so fatigued they felt like they were on fire—and just made it over when the wave started to break. I was dragged backward and sucked into the exploding lip so fast I didn't have time to take a lasting breath. I came as close as I ever have to drowning. When I surfaced, choking, the next wave was already breaking. I instinctively ditched my board to swim beneath the wave—something I swore I'd never, ever do. But it happened before I knew it and was probably the only reason I made it out.

Kurt was waiting for me halfway back to the boat. He grimaced when I approached. "That looked brutal."

I was so tired and frazzled that I felt shaky, sick almost. "Yeah," I said.

"How 'bout a beer?" His kind eyes warmed me from the inside out.

I sighed hard to shake off the demons. "Maybe a nap," I replied with a weak smile.

———————————|———————————

Our resort promised access to six local waves daily, but after our arrival we quickly discovered that only two actually break on a regular basis. Since Resorts was the first, that left Mini Pipe, a super-shallow, hollow left known to break boards and filet surfers. When I asked other guests about the remaining four waves, no one had surfed them. Most didn't even know they existed; they had all come to surf Frigates Passage, the only non-local wave, an exquisite offshore reef located an hour away by fast boat, or, when that wasn't possible, they'd settle for Pipe.

Pictures of Frigates Passage covered the walls of the resort's reception area. The wave reminded me of photos I'd seen of Cloud-break and Hawaii's famous Pipeline: perfectly formed barrels with a tiny surfer tucked inside. I knew there was no way I had the skills to surf Frigates, but I wanted at least to see it. If I signed up for the all-day trip, I could use the safe channel as my own front-row seat to watch some truly excellent surfers up close.

Unfortunately, access to Frigates was dictated by a combination of tide cycle, sunrise, and swell and wind predictions. After a few days, it seemed like the resort used any excuse not to make the trip. The surfers got antsy, and the evenings around the resort bar became more and more lively. Without surfing, and with the remoteness of the resort, there was really nothing else to do but drink.

Kurt and I got to know a group of guys from Colorado. Clem, Jason, and Chip worked in the ski industry during the winter, saving every penny in order to splurge on surf trips in the off-season. Chip, a redhead with a real job on his horizon, told me that sometimes, in the dead of winter, they got so surf-crazy that they'd pile into one car and blaze south to Baja for a long weekend. "It's not that bad," he said to my surprised look. "We take turns driving. Once, we even took our girlfriends." Despite their lack of consistent wave-time, they were gifted surfers.

I got to know Chip during a boat trip to Mini Pipe. The wind was howling, churning the water into frothy whitecaps, but the resort offered to take a group out for a look anyway. I planned to snorkel while Kurt and the other guests surfed. One of the guests commented on how the wave would probably be blown out, and that we'd all be better off with dive gear.

"You a diver?" one of the ski bums asked this other guest.

"I've done a little," he replied. "You guys?"

Tall, quiet Clem just shook his head no. Jason, whose shock of blonde hair was so crusty with salt it seemed to always stand on end, said he wanted to but hadn't gotten around to it. Everybody then looked at Chip, who was digging in his backpack for sunscreen. He came up smiling, and guffawed, "No. But I'm a muff diver!"

There were a few chuckles until suddenly all eyes turned to me, the only girl in the boat.

Chip's face went from an already pinkish tinge to mahogany red. His jaw dropped open and he stammered, "I . . . I'm sorry." He swallowed hard, with eyes wide. "I'm not used to there being girls out here."

It was true—despite surfing's recent boom among women, at that time it was still rare to see more than a few women in the lineup, especially in hard-to-reach places like Fiji, but I was no stranger to being in the minority. As an outdoor school instructor, as a backcountry skier and mountain climber, even as a science teacher, I was usually the lone female.

Mini Pipe turned out to be blown out, with ripping currents and a crappy, side-shore wind, but the surfers gave it a try anyway. In the end, they were envious of my snorkel gear and I ended up letting a few of them use it.

————————|————————

After a few more days surfing Resorts with only marginal improvement in my abilities, we finally got our chance to visit Frigates. The predictions called for swell in the four-foot range—a tiny version of the beast. Everybody was bummed and many surfers backed out the morning of the trip. But I was more eager than ever. Maybe I wouldn't have to spend the day watching and snorkeling. Maybe the small swell would make Frigates mellow enough for me to surf.

The resort used a special boat to get to Frigates, one with twin engines for extra speed and with beefier safety equipment because the reef is like a needle in a haystack, miles from any shore. Despite the prediction for calm seas, the ride was bumpy and rough, with spray blasting in from the sides, dousing everybody. I arrived soaked, with bruised kidneys and a sore butt. To my surprise, there were several other boats parked in the channel. From one, a pair of surfers jumped over the side and paddled toward the wave, their heads and shoulders swaying in time with their strokes.

"Holy cow," I said. The sun had barely risen above the horizon and there were already this many people? I could have sworn I'd read about our resort's exclusive rights to all the breaks. We hadn't yet shared waves with anyone during our stay—the whole idea behind traveling halfway across the world and paying good money was no crowds. Where had these other boats come from, Mars?

Next to me, Chip shrugged. "Any joker with a boat can get here."

My shoulders sagged. The thought of having to compete for waves with forty Kelly Slaters crushed my spirits. My dejection deepened when two more boats pulled up while our driver finished anchoring ours. After a quick scan of the channel and takeoff zone, I counted thirty surfers. With the addition of our group and the latest arrivals, we would be well into the fifties.

The only good news was the wave: the long paddle gave me a chance to assess the danger, and as far as I could see, it was minimal. Frigates Passage, for all its hype, looked mellow and fun. The small swell had transformed it into a gutless, slow-to-crumble wave, perfect for longboarding. I was elated. And the conditions were gorgeous: cloudless sky, no wind, and clear water shimmering over a pristine reef. In my dreams I could not have imagined better.

Reality set in as I neared the takeoff, where the atmosphere turned downright frosty. All the surfers were men, and all straddled shortboards, the tiny, thin, pointy-tipped variety that take years to learn how to ride. The surfers wore red rashguards, black ones, loud neon ones, and board shorts of all lengths and designs. I could hear Spanish, Italian, and Aussie twang. Frigates was living up to its reputation as a worldwide draw. But I was confused. What could this wave offer shortboarders that day? The waves were slow, mushy, and mellow. Why had none of them traded their potato chips for a tanker? Were they waiting for that one rogue wave to give them the ride their mounts deserved? Or did they enjoy scratching and clawing their way into waves that didn't have the speed to carry them?

Slowly, I recognized the reason for the chilly reception. With longboards (mine and Kurt's) now in the mix, their balance was upended. Because longboards can catch waves earlier, Kurt and I paddled to a location farther outside than the shortboarders—this meant we could drop into waves *before* the shortboarders. Essentially, if I had wanted to be an asshole, I could have taken any wave I wanted and run over anyone who got in my way.

But I am not an asshole. At least I wasn't until that day.

I let what I thought was a reasonable number of waves pass, out of respect. So when I paddled for my first wave, I expected the crowd to back off. But it was as if I didn't exist. The shortboarders were like a pack of sharks, each for themselves. If I paddled for a wave, ten other surfers paddled, too. If I went to drop in, I'd see three shortboarders below me and have to pull out or risk skewering them.

After two hours of this total frustration, I was forced to release my inner wildcat and call off the surfers in my path. Finally, I got a wave to myself.

And what did I do?

I pearled. Straight down, nose first, my feet flipping over my head and my board popping skyward like a cork.

Right in front of every cocky shortboarder in the water.

I *pearled*.

Besides wanting to scream, I was so embarrassed that I wanted to sink beneath the surface and live with the fish forever.

I hadn't pearled since I was a beginner. How on earth had this happened? To make matters worse, my rashguard got rolled up to my armpits in the thrashing that followed, taking my bikini top with it. I suppose I am just destined to be a flasher.

I knew my wave-catching at Frigates was over. No one would let me have any waves after that. They would consider it a waste of a wave because the kooky girl would surely pearl or somehow flub it up again. I had no choice but to retire to the boat.

I passed the remaining hours snorkeling, beating myself up repeatedly for my mistake, but little by little the beauty of the reef distracted me from my grief. Frigates Passage contained a veritable undersea wilderness: schools of huge, blue-finned tuna hunkered in the crevices of the nubby reef; tiny yellow minnow guys darted beneath purple cabbage heads of coral; big-mouthed, multicolored fish with fins that looked as delicate as butterfly wings sat like fat cats, waiting for lunch to blow by. I listened to the constant crackling of the living reef being moved by the current, like a million tiny mouths eating Fritos. I let my body float with the pulses of swell, dampened after their journey over the reef. I dove beneath the surface and lost myself in the serenity and splendor.

I expected to be shunned by our group of surfers after my performance, treated like the kook I thought I was. But something was different after that morning. As surfers trickled in from the surf that afternoon, they gravitated to the bow where I was trying to hide. Beers and snacks were passed around, and there were stories and laughter.

Maybe I had earned some brownie points for my attempts at Frigates, or maybe this new acceptance grew from something Chip had said to me earlier in the trip. While surfing at Resorts, I had dropped in on a wave just as the boat to Frigates Passage cruised through the channel. With all eyes on me, I had fallen, even plugged my nose before the wave swallowed me—an instinct I had not yet learned to control. That night on the resort's patio, cold Fiji Bitters sweating in our hands, Chip had said to me, his eyes sincere, "That was awesome, seeing you drop in on that bomb." No mention of my fall or my embarrassing nose-clamping.

Whatever the reason, after that day at Frigates, those surfers looked me in the eyes. I felt like I was one of them.

———————+———————

After a death-defying taxi to the main airport followed by a ride in a twin-engine plane in which our surfboards rode like passengers, Kurt and I landed at a gravel airstrip populated by wild chickens. Kadavu Island is shaped like the spine of a *Brachiosaurus* and is home to a world-class diving spot called the Astrolabe. It was also the access point for our next surfing destination. Tiny and beachless, Nagigia (pronounced na-Neen-ya) could be a lava bomb spit from Kadavu's highest peak, King Kong Mountain (the same as seen in the original film).

From the airstrip, Kurt and I buddy-carried our duffels and coffinlike board bag across the island's only road to an empty, white-sand beach where an open skiff waited in the shallows. A thin man wearing a faded canvas bucket hat, loose-fitting pants, and rubber flip-flops introduced himself as Ratu ("but you can call me Roger," he said with a humble smile) and helped us load our gear. Because Ratu-Call-Me-Roger was dark-skinned but not Fijian, I surmised that he must be East Indian, descended from the indentured laborers originally brought to Fiji to harvest sugar cane (Fijians were understandably not keen on such backbreaking work). After their tenure as laborers ended, many Indians decided to stay and today make up a good percentage of the population.

Once we broke away from the shallow lagoon near the airport, Ratu's counterpart, a stout and seemingly mute Fijian, opened the throttle and soon we were racing past beaches so white they blinded me. The cool ocean air felt delicious on my cheeks after the stuffy plane ride. As we curved outside of a patch of reef, a school of flying fish leapt from the sea, hovering for a magic instant, their golden scales glistening in the sun. As we traced the western edge of Kadavu, I spotted our destination: a scruffy brown rock edged with swaying palm trees. It looked like a gumdrop with fur.

When our boat driver slowed the boat to cross a shockingly bright turquoise lagoon, I heard what sounded like song. Squinting at the island's landing, I noticed that it was packed with swaying Fijians, the women dressed in long batik dresses and with flowers in their dark hair, the men in Hawaiian-style shirts playing guitars.

"They are singing," Ratu said with a shy smile. I looked around— who were they serenading? Was somebody getting married?

Ratu seemed to read my mind. "They are singing for *you*," he said.

The loveliness of the gesture overwhelmed me. It was a welcome song, full of harmony and sweetness, and I was deeply touched.

The song reached its finale as bow ropes were thrown around cleats and we were helped onto the dock. We were introduced to everyone and shook hands all the way up the stairs. We were led down tidy, crushed-shell pathways lined with tiki-torches to our *bure*, a thatched-roof cabin complete with its own outdoor shower and wraparound deck. I walked through the simple room to the patio overlooking the lagoon. The receding tide barely covered a spiky carpet of an expansive, rust-colored reef. At the far edge of this reef stood a village with tin-roofed buildings set among tall palms and a soccer field at its edge. "That is Nabukulevu-i-Ra," Ratu said. "At low tide you can walk there, across the reef, if you wish."

Kurt and I continued on to the main building of the resort, which sat on stilts and where we were invited for a late lunch. We stepped onto the large wraparound deck and rounded the side of the building, passing two bathrooms and a few tiny guest rooms to an expansive patio set beneath overhanging shade banners. Over the tops of gently swaying palms was the entire southern sea and fringing reef. I saw a distant wave peeling and realized that I must be looking at King Kong Left, the resort's jewel, and I muttered a rapturous, "Ohhhhh." Next to me, Kurt blinked; his mouth hung slightly open.

To an observer, we must have looked shell-shocked. After a week-plus of frustrating guesswork about the surf conditions, here was our own personal bird's-eye view. There were even binoculars handy for close-ups. I later discovered that an even closer view could be had from the island's rocky tip, easily reached via a short hike. Access to the surf was still boat-only, but the drivers ran shuttles all day, so we wouldn't be committed to spending an entire morning out on the open sea. Forgot sunscreen? Want to try a different board? Need a snack? No problem, we'll just whisk you back to the resort and when you're ready, it's back to the waves in a jiffy. I couldn't believe our luck: all the things we'd longed for at our previous spot existed at Nagigia. Even the conditions had come together. Despite my constant dread of surfing powerful waves, I was itching to get in the water.

"Duuudes," a familiar voice called out from behind us. I turned to see the normally stoic Clem grinning from ear to ear. "Welcome to Paradise," he added. He was laid out on a couch inside an open-air living room while groovy down-beat music played from a compact stereo system. "You're gonna like it here," he said in his normal understated way before disappearing behind the couch again.

I had known it was only a matter of time before we would run into one of the guys—their itinerary was almost identical to ours. "Where are Chip and Jason?" I asked. I was envious now of their two-day lead at paradisiacal Nagigia. I found out later that a perfect swell had been lighting up every reef in sight, with zero wind and sunny skies, so that at high tide the resort became a ghost town; everybody was in the water.

Clem gave us a dismissive wave from the back of the couch, as if to say, "Who cares?"

Because of the lowering tide, the waves would soon be shut down for the day so Kurt and I idled away the afternoon snorkeling, exploring the island's rocky coastline (no sticky brown mud in sight), and getting our boards ready for the surf the following day.

Besides King Kong Left, a powerful but still slightly forgiving wave, Nagigia offered access to several others. One, called Daku, was apparently perfect for longboarding. The next morning saw the island buzzing with amped surfers—the conditions were perfect and everybody was in a rush to get to the waves. Breakfasts were scarfed, boards were thrown into boats, and sunscreen was hastily smeared in thick patches that made us look like a tribe of displaced natives.

For the first time during the trip, I was not the only woman heading out to surf. Joined by Shasta, a honeymooner new to surfing, and Emily, a solo traveler from California needing a break from the heavy King Kong Left, we hopped aboard a skiff and soon were careening toward friendly Daku. We passed Nagigia's rocky southern edge, the smooth unbroken ocean expanding off to what seemed like the end of the world. Rounding Nagigia, I got the first waterline view of King Kong Left. It was living up to its reputation, pumping out clean, glassy waves big enough to dwarf a school bus. Our driver kept us well outside but close enough to the surfers bobbing in a tight cluster at the takeoff for me to feel like I was part of the action. In a burst of speed, one surfer paddled into a huge curling wave. I caught a glimpse of him speeding down the line before the advancing wave's wall blocked him from view. A few moments later he emerged, releasing a fan of spray as he launched over the lip. It could have been a scene from a surf movie. I envied these surfers their ability, but I think I had the most fun of anyone that day at Daku.

Leaving King Kong Left in our wake, our driver traced the edge of the reef to a quiet cove facing an empty, white-sand beach. Slender palms with droopy green leaves arced over water so still and clear it could have been a swimming pool; beneath the surface, heads of dark coral clustered like giant marbles on the pale-sand ocean bottom. Long, smooth lines of swell rose up and folded so softly they made almost no sound. If not for our ever-limiting tide window, I would have liked to sit and soak in every gorgeous detail. But I was out of the boat in a flash.

I paddled into a wave that held me gently and whispered instead of roared. I trailed my hand behind me in the tropical water, playing notes of joy in the slippery, salty ocean curling around my fingers. I felt like the star of my very own surf story. With just me and the other girls, there were plenty of waves to go around and I wasted no time in between them, paddling back out with my eyes on my next wave. I stroked into countless waves, easing onto the gentle face and gliding along until it faded out in the channel. Shasta, Emily, and I developed a natural rotation, and for the first time I understood how easy it was to get greedy: when conditions and ability come together in a perfectly matched setting, the temptation to take more than one's share of the waves is difficult to ignore. Each wave felt like a gift, and when it was time to go I ignored the patient Fijian waiting for me in the boat for as long as I could. It was heartbreaking to leave. I pictured myself surfing that wave every day, my confidence growing, my skills improving, until the final day when I would make my breakthrough debut at King Kong Left.

Such was not to be, as in so many surf stories, because the conditions did an about-face. With the approach of a low-grade typhoon, the ocean became a frothy, swirling mess. So violent was the weather, in fact, that the sunny patio was closed after a loose sun shade broke free and smashed one of the living room windows. After that, we were forced to eat our meals inside the cramped, stuffy living room.

And the surf? Most days we were lucky to get a few waves at Namo, a choppy, shallow, and sectiony wave that sucked the reef dry at its end. Besides lamenting what we had lost, Kurt and I and the rest of the marooned guests spent many afternoons playing ping-pong, watching surf videos, and of course, drinking Fiji Bitters. King Kong Left still worked occasionally, but it was a sinister, darker version of itself, with strong, funky currents and lopsided faces, and I only paddled out once. I shouldn't have bothered; I sat there like a buoy. So much for my debut.

As the stormy days stretched on, I thought back to my first days at Resorts. I couldn't help wishing that I'd pushed myself harder then, when the conditions had been favorable. As well, I should have stayed out at Frigates and elbowed my way past the sneering looks and cold shoulders to take another wave, and another. Had I squandered my chance to transform into the surfer I wanted to be by thinking I had weeks of good waves to work up my courage?

However melancholy I felt about my surfing, the fickle surf and stormy days gave Kurt and me time to explore the island and its surroundings. As well, we had the pleasure of befriending some of the Fijians who worked at the resort (and who all lived in the village I had seen across the reef). Every morning, despite horrible wind and currents, I would hear them arrive via boat to the dock below our *bure*. Instead of keeping the grumpy silence of a begrudging worker starting their day at 5:00 AM, they sang softly and giggled, speaking to each other in playful, chatty voices. We were invited many times to their village, where we were treated like royalty. Once, we observed one of the matriarchs paint tapas, a rapidly declining paper art using traditional inks. We visited the village's kava fields where young men were in the middle of hand-harvesting the hearty root from a sloping dirt field. The aging Fijian in charge of the operation told us he exported to places as far away as Germany. I looked around and tried to imagine this fellow—with no phone, no Internet, no running water, even, closing deals with German businesses. And we played volleyball—not the competitive and highly organized form of the sport, but the Fijian hybrid in which anyone can switch sides at any time, teams are of uneven numbers, and matchpoint can be eleven, twenty-four, or a hundred. When the ball soared out of bounds, everybody laughed.

Despite the frustration of spending a week on a barren island with stormy or no surf, leaving would prove difficult. I'm not sure when it happened, but Fiji's relaxed pace had gotten under my skin. Had surfing done this to me? All those moments of sitting in the water, waiting, slowing my mind in order to focus on the ocean's energy? Or was it the graceful Fijian hosts, whose moods didn't depend on what the winds were doing to the waves or whether or not they'd scored a sweet barrel ride the day before? I had stopped asking needy questions: *when* will the boat leave, *who* is going, *what* are the surf predictions for Tuesday? I had become comfortable with heeding the rhythms of the tide and enjoying simple pleasures—a warm shower, fresh food, good company, and maybe a chance to connect with a single pulse of energy rippling through the ocean. Was there a need for anything else?

---

I sat in the tiny shack of the airport terminal, glad to be alive after the most hair-raising boat taxi of my life. The massive swells had tossed our little boat in every direction and the wind had blown sea spray over us so many times I felt completely brined. At first, every time the boat slammed into a trough I cringed, thinking about my treasured longboard snapping in two, but after we had reached the open sea I became much more worried about the structural integrity of our boat. I imagined the three of us abandoning ship with no life vests or signaling equipment, becoming separated, cold, tired, and either washing over the reef or getting dragged out to sea. My hands had gripped the gunnels like vises and were still cramped and clawlike. Our boat driver, a Fijian of few words named Manu, had taken it all in stride, even smiling out of the side of his raincoat hood. After dropping us off, he headed into the storm again, but not before tossing us a big grin and a one-arm wave, his huge hand open, fingers wide, like a baseball mitt waiting for a pop fly.

When we checked in and handed over our board bags, the airport official told us that the next plane was ours. This surprised me, as I had yet to meet a Fijian who cared if anything was on time; in fact, I had decided weeks ago to ditch my watch so I could better adapt.

I was ready to go home, but the end of a trip like that is always hard for me. My belly craves treats like aged cheddar and toaster waffles, but my heart wants to stay. I felt different, like I'd shed old habits that distracted from the happiness at the heart of good, clean living. It was as if I had molted, and I was scared that my new skin would be too delicate against the frantic melee of city noises and people in a hurry. How could I keep this new piece of me—the one that didn't rely on email and lavender-scented soap—from getting trampled in the real world?

Soon a small plane drifted in, its wings barely clearing the airport's tin roof. I remembered the official's pledge—the next plane would be ours—but I knew better, so I waited. Sure enough, once the arriving passengers cleared the runway, the plane buttoned up and sped downwind with enough alacrity to scare the scavenging chickens. I stole a glance at the official who nodded reassuringly. "*Next* plane is your plane," he said with certainty. I shrugged, unconcerned. Our connecting flight in Nadi did not leave until late evening. I sat back and closed my eyes.

I was pulled from a pleasant doze by the sound of a plane's approach. I opened one eye and saw the official, who confirmed that this was our plane. Curious, I peered through the open doorway to see the same plane from earlier touch down. But instead of stopping, the single prop raged along the dusty landing strip for a few moments then departed, lifting on wobbling wings. I arched an eyebrow at the official.

"Next plane," he said with the same frank nod.

I dug out my book but soon the plane's touch-and-go scenario repeated, only this time from the opposite direction. I began to chuckle when the official again made his promise. I realized he was like other Fijians I had met on that trip: so concerned for my contentment he would say or do anything to provide it, even make up answers to questions he personally thought were pointless. I realized he had no idea when my plane would arrive, nor did he know what time the bank opened or what was for dinner.

Our plane eventually landed and while the luggage was loaded, I fished out my neglected watch and figured that I'd better get used to wearing it again. But it remained cradled in my hands, its digital numbers clicking efficiently by. The official waited by the gate with Kurt, who was fixing me with a perplexed look. I placed the watch on the seat, as if to make an offering to the portal that had so affected me. I knew it was silly; leaving a watch behind didn't mean I'd be able to live in our modern world without keeping time. But maybe, when waiting in line for coffee or sitting in a crowded lineup of surfers feeling impatient for a wave, instead of sighing in exasperation I'd remember this moment. I'd remember riding waves at breathtaking Daku or laughing with the Fijians on the volleyball court.

Hopefully, I would remember that time could slow down if I let it.

# 5

# CANADIAN GIRLS GONE WILD IN BAJA

IF I COULD CHOOSE the circumstances of my first-ever hitchhike, I would not be alone, it would not be pouring down rain, and it would not be in a country famous for its banditos. I'd also know the language (I will forever hold a grudge against my seventh grade homeroom teacher for recommending *French* over Spanish).

I had arrived in Todos Santos travel-beaten and half a day late after fleeing a winter so wet my entire town flooded and so disastrously stormy I hadn't surfed in months. In a gigantic leap of faith, I had recently quit my teaching job so I could follow my dream of being a travel writer. I justified the trip to Baja as a chance to be "on assignment"; an actual message I debated adding to an out-of-office response on my email, even though the "assignment" existed only in my head. In reality, I was being allowed to tag along on a yoga and surf retreat organized by my friend Jenny Stewart, founder of Surf Sister, who had partnered with Shani Cranston, a fellow Canadian and espouser of wellness retreats. Shani, a dedicated natural-food chef would provide the meals; Lou, a Surf Sister instructor, would lead the surfing lessons; and Marne, a yogini from LA would be our yoga diva. I paid for my own airfare and travel expenses (dipping into my rapidly dwindling savings) and gratefully accepted a break on the cost of the retreat, agreeing to camp on the beach instead of staying in the rented house, which was already full of paying guests from as far away as the Midwest. I planned to get photos and witty quotes from the other retreat attendees and sell the story to *Outside* magazine or *Yoga Journal*. As for surfing, I hoped Lou might offer me a few pointers.

As a bonus, after the retreat ended, Louise and Shani would meet up with Jenny and the majority of the Surf Sister instructors venturing from Vancouver Island for a surf rendezvous at a villa they'd rented a little ways up the coast from the yoga retreat. Would I like to join them? This seemed like a dream come true: surf alongside star surfer girls in warm water? Plus, I was combining my love for surfing with writing. Maybe I could create a story about the Surf Sister surfari, too. In my mind, I was well on my way to free trips to Peru or Croatia to write for *Budget Travel* or my favorite, *National Geographic Adventure*. Naïve? Completely. But that didn't stop me from charging forward with all cylinders firing.

My thus-far easy travel took a turn for the worse after landing in Cabo's airport to discover that the only way to reach my bus connection north was to hitch a ride on the shuttle headed for the overdeveloped hotel strip. Packed with party-hungry tourists throwing their newly converted pesos at the bus driver, the shop owner from whom they bought tequila, and the shady lady selling made-in-China finger puppets, the worst part was listening to the perky guide who tried to sell us a time-share. They dropped me at a dusty bus depot and drove off singing, "Ninety-nine bottles of beer on the wall . . . " while I scrambled to find my connection. Halfway into my bus journey north it began to rain and the normally dry washes filled with red-brown rivers that spilled over the road, delaying us. Once I was in Todos Santos, my prearranged ride didn't show and I was forced to haggle for a night's stay in a seedy hotel populated by a family of mice that ate through my backpack and left little brown turds in my underwear. "You've gotta go," Kurt had encouraged me even though we'd be apart. Now I wondered if I'd made a mistake.

In the morning I called the emergency phone number listed in my paperwork and ended up speaking not with the yogini I had been scheduled to meet the evening before, but with the owner of the house where the yoga/surf retreat was taking place. He was a gringo in Cabo, who, between drags from what I imagined was a fat reefer, called me "dude" and informed me that the house I so wanted to reach had no phone. "But, you know, it's only like . . . (inhale) . . . (then, with pinched breath) . . . ten kilometers (exhale). You should just walk, dude."

*Walk?* How? Along the freeway? Where speeding semis regularly ran cars off the road? Was he nuts?

"Or, wait! Dude! You're in Todos! Just hitchhike. *Nooo* problem."

Hitchhike? Yeah, right! Besides the obvious dangers of bumming a ride in a foreign country, I didn't even know where I was going, precisely. It was a beach called San Pedritos, but who knew which random dirt road off the freeway led there—it's not like Mexico is known for its accurate signage.

I gave walking a go. After all, I've backpacked with thigh-burning loads for weeks on end, up the sides of mountains. Ten kilometers was nooo problem. But I hadn't even cleared the last taco stand when my shoulder started screaming for mercy and a deep ache settled into my chest bones. It was the nine-foot board bag slung over my shoulder, stuffed with not just my longboard but also my sleeping bag and tent for extra padding (airline baggage handlers are about as careful with fragile surfboards as the average gorilla). All together, it probably weighed no more than twenty pounds, but carrying a loaded board bag is like portaging a canoe: it doesn't get heavy until after it's too late to abandon it. I soon wished I'd taken up fly fishing. Plus in my genius I'd decided to bring the "travel" pack, whose skinny straps give my hips welts and, when loaded, rides like a bundle of overactive yams. Then, the light mist turned to hard, cold rain.

Banditos or not, hitchhiking started sounding pretty good.

And of all things, an American picked me up. A surfer, too, with a pretty good bead on the local beaches.

----------------+----------------

An hour later, the driver inched his rented van across the barren arroyo. If not for the previous winter's Hurricane Marty, the place would have been packed with tents, motor homes, lawn chairs, ATVs, and feral children pinballing through it all, high on orange Fanta. As the van approached a big, pink house, a group of people gathered at the corner of the broad, open-air deck.

My escort stuck his head out the window. "Yoga?" he asked.

They got excited. "Yeah!"

Within an hour I was deep into my first real yoga class. Our instructor, Marne, a petite brunette from California with zero body fat, led us through poses and told me how to breathe through my nose. I was challenged and stretched and when I was done, felt exhilarated. I couldn't wait to do it again.

Most of the week was spent practicing yoga, as the post-hurricane wave at San Pedritos wasn't quite the same and was definitely too burly for most of the surfers in our group. Plus, most of the retreat guests had never surfed before, so Lou's lesson resembled the one I'd received from Karen and I didn't get much out of it. But by the end of the retreat, I felt like I was standing up straight for the first time in my life. My arms, from countless Vinyasas, felt strong, too. I was itching to join up with the Surf Sisters to catch some warm-water waves.

Car doors slammed, girls' voices barked hurriedly at each other, the gate was opened, and we were off. I was crammed into a rented minivan with a group of rabid surfers, some who had never surfed without a wetsuit. There had not even been time for introductions; I was simply swept up in their tornado on the way to the waves. The winds were dying and we were chasing a rumor of an evening glass-off at La Pastora, a sandy beach just north of the rented villa Jenny's crew had seized for the week.

Chasing was what it felt like, riding with our possessed madwoman of a driver. Beyond the town, Andrea rammed over speed hurdles and skidded around corners so forcefully that I wished I had brought a helmet. While her foot pinned the gas pedal to the floor, her blonde copilot blared unruly indie-punk and sang along at full volume, head bobbing, her twin ponytails a blur as we bounced and lurched. My hands were glued to the ceiling to keep two surfboards (swinging upside-down from a hastily assembled rope sling) from crashing onto my head. We turned onto a deserted dirt road and Andrea yelled, "Hold on!" The van accelerated toward a huge puddle of unknown depth and I fearfully let go of the cargo above me to brace myself. At impact, a wall of murky water exploded up past the windows and sloshed over the hood.

I was still picking surf wax out of my hair as I followed the Surf Sisters as they bolted to the beach for a surf check. I got there just as they turned around to rush back for their boards, practically squealing. When I stepped up to the berm I understood why. Framed by an empty crescent of caramel-colored beach, the azure Pacific spread endlessly before me. The wind had indeed died off and waves peeled from a broad point made of cabbage-sized cobbles the color of slate. A handful of surfers were in the water, hunched like crows on a wire as they waited for waves. I watched one drop in and dance like a shadow in front of its frothy, lime-green lip. Even though the waves looked at least head-high, which was still big for me, they emitted a gentle, frothy kind of rumble and crumbled more than broke. No booming. No exploding over a dicey tropical reef. I was positively giddy.

The Surf Sisters continued to move like a flock of little birds, twittering and rushing here and there and then racing back to the beach. They were in the lineup before I could get a fresh coat of wax on my board. In a world usually dominated by men, it was fantastic to think of these crackerjack women surfers taking over a lineup, and I was sorry I missed it. After paddling out, I sat on the outside for a long time, anxious about the possibility of flailing in front of the Surf Sisters and still haunted by the fears that lingered from Fiji. When finally I caught a wave, I was ecstatic, my bare feet gripping the waxy deck of my board. My week of yoga had paid off; I felt fit and healthy, as if my spine had been replaced with a young alder bough. I heard laughter from the Surf Sisters drift over the tops of the waves. I listened to Andrea explain her atypical surf attire (a pair of blue nylon shin-length pants) to a stranger: "They're called the shants because they're not shorts, they're not pants . . . they're shants, eh?" I watched the women dominate—no timid Marys among them—and secretly wished for their confidence, their experience.

The sun sank low and the girls each took their last wave. I followed, feeling stoked about the days to come. As I crested the berm, bright forks of lightning flashed over the distant mountains, dark with heavy curtains of rain. I turned back for one last look at the ocean and found its surface an inky gloss highlighted with crimson and gold.

During the drive home, Andrea threaded through narrow, sandy streets and over warped roads, then suddenly cranked the wheel to stop at a small *mercado,* its bright overhead lights illumi-nating dusty, sparsely filled shelves. One Surf Sister emerged from the store with a huge package of toilet paper. "Do you *know* how much toilet paper a house of girls will go through in a week?" she asked me with one eyebrow arched. Andrea's punk-loving wingman followed, holding a bag of animal crackers big enough to choke an alligator. "In case we get stranded," she informed me through a mouthful.

We arrived at our small villa just as darkness settled in. After the boards and belongings were stowed, we entered the kitchen where Shani was orchestrating a feast. Her yoga retreat successfully completed, she had moved over to the Sisters' camp to be our chef for the week. Instantly, my taste buds ached with anticipation as wafts of curry and coriander drifted past my nose. As Shani put the finishing touches on a meal fit for a goddess, the rest of the Sisters hovered, ravenous, and swapped highlights from their session.

Just before dawn the next morning, I was pulled from sleep by what sounded like palm trees fluttering in the breeze. I was camped in the spacious yard inside the villa and from between the flaps of my tent I saw only limp leaves—everything was com-pletely still. Curious, I listened more closely. Could the noise be coming from waves?

Whoa.

The word spread like wildfire and soon everyone was out of bed and bustling. The villa was awash with the sounds of girls stacking boards on roof racks and shouting to each other to hurry up in the bathroom.

Jenny took the wheel that day, and at one point the road passed a viewpoint of the waves below. Neat, perfectly spaced lines of swell were stacked to the horizon like sharp ridges of corduroy; I could see the offshore wind shearing plumes of spray from the backs of the blue green waves as they curled forward and peeled the length of the beach. We sat in reverence for a moment, then let out a collective "Wowwww," before Jenny got friendly with the accelerator.

———————————|———————————

Our excitement ebbed when we saw the waves up close: fifteen-foot walls barreled like freight trains from way outside the point. Only a handful of surfers were out despite many vehicles parked at the edge of the berm. We watched one surfer paddle out: after waiting for a lull he quickly picked his way over the boulders and leapt forward, paddled like hell, and in an instant was swept down the beach. After taking several waves on the head and finally clearing the impact zone, he was a half a mile down from the takeoff.

The surf was too serious for me, too serious for the dozen other would-be surfers standing along the edge of the shore. I was eager to see the Surf Sisters racing into the waves, sand kicking up from their heels. But all soles stood firmly planted; they looked on with arms crossed tight, faces stoic. After some discussion, a few—Andrea, Jenny, Lou, and Shani—decided to stay; maybe the swell would drop or a change in tide would dampen the current. The rest of us decided to check out a smaller-wave alternative down the coast. We left with heavy hearts.

Over the next few days the hammering swell dropped bit by bit, and the Sisters fell into a rhythm of exploring the coast for the best waves by day and eating Shani's fabulous cooking by night. But the final morning of the trip we again woke to the sound of booming surf and decided to head to the hurricane-ravaged San Pedritos.

As we neared the beach, it became clear that this was no ordinary big swell—exploding waves shook the ground. My jaw dropped to the floor as macking, thick-lipped barrels roared at us, spitting spray from their bellies as they spun and folded. Spent waves receding over the cobbles sounded like Godzilla sucking down a Slurpee.

"I'm not goin' out there!" Jenny cried. No stranger to power-ful waves, Jenny has been all over the world and started surfing when she was a kid. Needless to say, I sided with Jenny. A carload of girls opted for Los Cerritos and quickly departed; I couldn't resist the chance to watch Andrea and Shani charge the big stuff and settled in along the rocks with my camera.

Andrea took the first wave, a glassy, indigo blue wall laced with pearly foam that arched up like the wing of a giant raptor. During her paddle back out, she was stuffed deep during a duck-dive and then pinned to the bottom of the ocean by a boulder that somehow got rolled over her foot. Days later she would discover that the lingering soreness came from a broken metatarsal. But when she finally came in that day, it was because of a ripped leash plug—not because of the pain. With big, bright eyes and a huge grin, Andrea told me, "That was the best wave of my life!" Shani took several waves in her smooth, graceful manner, making surf-ing such giants look easy.

By the end of the Surf Sister getaway, I was savoring the rare treat of being surrounded by strong female surfers. Even though I had done more sitting in the lineup than surfing, their determina-tion, skill, and electric energy inspired me. It was also good to realize that even experienced surfers have limits. It made me feel a little bit better about Fiji, where so often I felt like a coward. Most of the Surf Sisters hadn't paddled out at Pedritos that last day, but it didn't make them any less skilled. At the end of the day, they were still good surfers.

When I called to thank Jenny again for such an awesome adventure, she mentioned that the following year's trip was already taking shape. "Kauai," Jenny said, taunting me. "It's going to be so fun!" As if I needed convincing. As I hung up the phone I could already feel my bare feet gripping my board, see the sparkling blue ocean, and hear the indie-punk blaring all the way to the beach.

# 6

# HOW TO SURF YOUR BRAINS OUT IN COSTA RICA

AFTER A DELUGE IN THE NIGHT left a lake at my doorstep, I woke on my first morning in Costa Rica to an opaque, brown ocean, like weak Folgers with too much cream. It looked disgusting. On top of that, the waves were lumpy, crappy, and small and pretty much like the most average beach break I had ever seen. I was not thrilled.

In fact, I was crushed. I had tossed and turned most of the night, worried that I'd made a mistake by coming to Witch's Rock Surf Camp. I had ignored the warnings (from Clem: "Costa Rica's all crappy beach breaks"; from Kurt: "Surf camps are for kooks") because I sensed there would be something special about this place, something more than met the eye. The possibility that I had been hoodwinked made me want to bury my head in the sand.

I had wanted to come to Costa Rica, and specifically to Witch's Rock Surf Camp in Tamarindo, so I could surf my brains out. Even though I no longer felt like a beginner, I wanted to speed up my learning curve. I was tired of my knees knocking when the swell was bigger than chest-high. I was tired of not feeling confident. A week of intense instruction would surely catapult my skills. Plus, after fickle Fiji, where we rarely surfed more than once a day, I practically drooled over the promise of double or even *triple* sessions. I imagined being so exhausted that by the end of the week the mere sight of a surfboard would make my limbs quiver. I also assumed that this surfing blitz would help calm my obsession. I rationalized that once I was able to surf at an acceptable level, I could relax about the whole thing and Kurt and I could get back to the business of having a normal married life. No more dragging him across the globe—putting a strain on our relationship and our finances—in order to surf.

So much for carefully laid plans.

———————————+———————————

Kurt and I stood side by side on a wide crescent of coarse brown sand with a local of slight build and fine cheekbones who ironically called himself Macho. His tightly curled hair seemed to spring from his head rather than grow from it.

"O-Keh," he said with his soft accent. "Now we surf."

Apparently Macho's job was to evaluate my surfing for the appropriate level of instruction. I was anxious about being watched—what if Macho thought I was hopeless? Nervously, I carried my board to the edge of the water and watched Macho paddle easily through the whitewash.

"Just have fun," Kurt said to me before following him.

I was both surprised and deeply glad for this encouragement. It meant that maybe Kurt didn't care that I had brought him to a surf camp where the waves were not azure blue and perfect but khaki brown and crappy. Or maybe he was at peace because for the next eight days he would be chauffeured to all of the best breaks as part of his enrollment in the camp's tours program. In fact, he was scheduled to leave in an hour for a place called Langosta with a guide named Abner. Maybe there the waves would be azure blue and perfect.

It meant that I could focus on surfing and try not to flunk out of the camp.

Paddling out with what I hoped looked like confident strokes, the water's warmth seemed to soothe my nerves and I made it to the lineup without getting my hair wet. A slight wind had kicked up, making the waves even messier than at first look, but after a few passed I saw one coming and spun for it. I managed to drop in and not fall or otherwise flub and was pleasantly puzzled to discover that the wave, unimpressive in appearance, had plenty of power but without being punchy. When I paddled back out, I was much more relaxed. The hope I felt when booking this trip, about there being a little bit of magic here, returned.

After a few more waves, Macho signaled us in. We stood on the shore with wet faces and bare feet sinking into the sugary sand, longboards tucked beneath our arms.

"No leh-ssons," Macho said.

My heart panged. No lessons? Had I failed? "What do you mean?" I asked.

"You just need to surf."

I imagined myself surfing that beach alone for a week while other guests were tutored nearby and Kurt was surfing his brains out somewhere up the coast.

Kurt frowned. "What's she going to do while I'm on tours?"

Macho gave him a curious look. "She can go tours, too."

The pronouncement hit me square in the chest: I was good enough for tours? Since when? I flipped through a mental slide show and saw myself flailing in Fiji, being skittish in Baja, and feeling frustrated in between in the fickle Northwest. "What about Witch's Rock?" I asked. The highlight of the tours experience was a day trip to the camp's namesake, a powerful A-frame wave located an hour's boat ride north. Wouldn't it be too heavy for me?

Macho shrugged. "You be fine."

Kurt and I exchanged glances. I saw that he was nervous for me, but he was also pleased. At least this way, we would be together.

———————|———————

I shook the hand of a shirtless, lanky youngster who introduced himself as Abner. He had a short mop of tightly curled hair, just like Macho, and looked not a day older than seventeen. His big brown eyes were soft and kind and his smile revealed sparkling white teeth. I soon developed a kind of maternal affection for these young surf guides and instructors, so full of playfulness and generosity and good manners; they made me feel like Wendy among Peter Pan's Lost Boys. Abner slid my longboard into his arms, and Kurt and I followed him out to the street where another guest was waiting by a rusty, compact SUV. Lickety-split, Abner was on the roof loading boards along with our driver, a stocky man named Wilfredo with laughing eyes and a mischievous grin.

The stifling midday humidity seemed to suck the oxygen from the air, and I was drenched in sweat. Being sandwiched between Kurt and Dillon, the other guest in the cramped SUV, felt like torture. The superheated air breezing through the windows offered little relief, and I quickly realized the only solution was to get in the water and stay there.

Costa Rica has two seasons, rainy and dry, and the difference between the two is drastic. We had arrived at the peak of the rainy season, when the hillsides sparkled with dewy green lushness and colors were so vibrant they exploded. Apparently, the small lake at my doorstep that morning was par for the course—it had been pouring every night and most afternoons. In fact, so much rain fell the previous week that a river literally ran through it—emptying from the street through the middle of the camp's open-air restaurant and out to sea. Because of all this moisture, we drove through the small town of Tamarindo on muddy, soupy streets, with slop spattering our vehicle's sides and windows. The town's only road dead-ended in a cul-de-sac of simple restaurants, ramshackle hotels, and a few souvenir shops. We turned left just before this and passed a large, glitzy surf shop that could have been airlifted from a densely populated California surf town. After passing the two-story glass monstrosity, the town seemed to fade into the jungle, with muddy side roads disappearing into dense green shadows and dilapidated vehicles clustered beneath thick, bushy trees.

I was nervous—what kind of wave was Langosta? Heavy? Mellow? Crowded? Was I going to make a fool of myself in front of Dillon and Abner? Would I get hurt?

During the drive, Dillon told us all about his job as a sound technician. After we parked in a tiny lot beneath a canopy of scraggly trees, he got out to type a text message on his phone and instructed Wilfredo to keep a close eye on his sandals, which he had bought while on tour with Soundgarden. Abner led us down a narrow path lined with tall grasses and low-hanging trees that had a rough, coffee-colored bark. The soft crush of breaking waves filtered through the scrub and I caught glimpses of sun-dappled ocean the same Folgers-brown as in Tamarindo. I chose not to look at Kurt to see if he was disappointed.

We broke through to a beach separated from the surf by a prickly jumble of dark rocks. I scanned the area, confused. The distant wave seemed to form outside of the rock-jumble. Were there submerged rocks out there, creating a pointlike setup? And where was the paddle-out? I imagined having to jump off the rock jumble without getting smashed against it and was scanning the horizon for another option when Abner pointed out a channel accessed from the beach, on the far side of the rocks.

Abner, Kurt, and Dillon discussed the wave while I watched a line of swell crest and begin to crumble. It looked okay, not *too* threatening but kind of big, maybe head-high. A little choppy.

Maybe a bit steep? In my mind I tried to recall all the advice I'd
ever received in order to prepare myself for my first-ever paddle
out as a non-newbie. From Karen: Cover my head in a wipeout and
paddle three more times before dropping in. From Captain Aloha:
Don't over-paddle or stand up straight. From the Surf Sisters: Just
because I was a girl didn't mean I had to surf like one. From the ski
bums in Fiji: Drop in on a big bomb and don't look back.

I took a big breath and waded forward, shuffling rather than
walking because apparently there were plenty of sharp rocks and
because the water was so brown my feet were invisible. The rest
of the group had already plunged through the whitewash and were
halfway to the lineup when I finally mounted my board and began
stroking hard for the outside.

The only difficult thing about getting outside was how long it
took me. The two other surfers in the water besides those in our
group, one Tico (what Costa Ricans call themselves) and one who
I guessed by the sunburn and racy board shorts was American,
did not give me more than a passing glance. I sat at the end of the
lineup feeling intimidated, taking stock of the scene while Kurt,
on the inside position, pivoted for a wave. He quickly pulled up,
however, to avoid Dillon, who blatantly snaked it. Dillon made the
drop and disappeared behind the curl.

While turning back to face the horizon, Kurt caught my eye
and angrily shook his head. Dillon exited his wave then paddled
around the breaker zone, past me to exactly where he came from,
inside of Kurt. I watched to see if Dillon offered some sort of
apology, but there was only silence. The atmosphere got tense. The
other two surfers were also taking the best waves for themselves.

Meanwhile Abner dropped in on all the scraps and rode them
with smooth, understated style. I would discover later that he
learned to surf only a few years prior, and on a shortboard. Talk
about a learning curve—most kids of similar ability would have

been surfing since kindergarten.

When Kurt claimed his next wave, the scenario with Dillon repeated. But he caught the following wave, and after a long ride, reappeared and caught up with Dillon. I heard the tail end of their conversation as they paddled past:

Kurt: "Maybe you could look around, is all I'm saying."

Dillon: "Oh, I saw you."

Kurt, perplexed: "Then why didn't you pull out?"

Dillon: "You didn't call me off, man." He paddled away and over his shoulder added, "Just call me off."

Kurt and Dillon separated to their corners. Later I asked Kurt why he didn't push the issue. "I'm a lover not a fighter," he said with a shrug.

As if this drama were not enough, I had yet to figure out the wave. The takeoff was steeper than it looked and there were a lot of close-outs, waves that wall up and collapse in one big dump. During my one good ride, I managed to drop in and stand, but the wall was so steep that I was sure it would close out, so I immediately exited and it was over before I could enjoy it. On my next wave I dropped in late and the crashing lip nearly split me in two, shoving me violently into the deep, then ripping me up to shove me down once more. I surfaced feeling completely worked and scared. When I finally built up the nerve to try again, Dillon was paddling directly below me, straining and kicking with his feet, thrashing like a fish out of water.

*Sigh.*

During the walk back to the car, the sounds of breaking waves blended with Dillon's "Why didn't you call me off, man?"

My head dropped to my chest. I had brought Kurt to a place where not only were the waves brown and crappy, but where he needed to call off kooks to ride them.

Dinner options at the camp's restaurant were expensive and Americanized, so we wandered across the street to a place called Rodamar, which had a cement floor, white plastic furniture, and a sign that read: "Typical Food." The open-air restaurant had only two other customers, a single Tico male and a plump, middle-aged Tico woman in an apron watching a plump, middle-aged Tico man eat. Kurt and I placed our order at a counter at the back. Shortly after, the Tico woman disappeared into the kitchen. My fried *camarones* were heaped high atop a plastic plate, the bed of rice beneath it browned and seasoned. Our young waiter delivered our food along with sets of white plastic silverware, all without removing his eyes from a soccer match playing on a flickering TV in the corner. Beyond the glow of overhead lights, the black, invisible jungle chirped with the sound of insects and breathed its hot, humid air against our necks.

Why anyone would call such mouth-watering food "typical" was beyond me. We ate like kings for pennies. Rodamar soon became our second home. I wondered if "typical" had been lost in translation on its way to "authentic." In any case, Costa Rica's typical food instantly became synonymous with "yum."

That night, I slept in air-conditioned bliss and woke wondering if the previous day's disappointment had all been a bad dream. I dressed in what by midweek would become my surf camp uniform: bikini, board shorts, t-shirt, flip-flops, then headed to the camp's restaurant without brushing my hair. On the way I swung by the chalkboard located above the front desk for a peek at the day's surf schedule. Kurt and I would be leaving for another rivermouth called Avellanas in half an hour, with a guide named Flash. Dillon, it seemed, had gone home.

An early morning squall had left the pavement steamy and the sky a misty blue. While Kurt and I helped load the boards, a tall

Tico with unkempt and uncharacteristically blonde hair coasted to the curb on a three-speed, a shortboard tucked under his arm. He was dressed only in a pair of orange and yellow surf trunks adorned with the bottom halves of thong-bikini-clad models, their perfectly round derrieres juxtaposed against the jagged black tops of palm trees. He spoke excitedly in Spanish to Wilfredo while flicking his right wrist—as if to pack an imaginary tin of tobacco—his knuckle joints kinking *snap! snap! snap!* This Tico then carefully slid his tiny board between the two front seats of the SUV, turned to us and said "*Vamanos?*" revealing a set of white, handsomely crooked teeth and sparkling, bright blue eyes. Wilfredo was already behind the wheel. Kurt and I shrugged at each other and got in.

When we pulled away from the camp, a young Tico on the street shot his fist skyward in salutation, yelling, "*pura vida!*" which translates literally into "pure life" but seems to resemble something closer to "life kicks ass, doesn't it!" Our blonde Tico leaned halfway out of the SUV to mimic the gesture, adding a battle cry that would wake the dead. Once back inside, he gave us the *pura vida* handshake: a slide of the palm, then a head-on fist bump. "I'm Flash," he said.

We drove north out of town and the pavement turned to hard-packed, pebbly dirt slicked with rain, the hand-dug gutters full of red brown water. We passed through a small village that smelled of fire-roasted peppers and cornmeal dough; a group of kids played soccer on a muddy side street. "Many of my frens come from here," Flash told us, nodding somberly.

Soon the tiny shacks and roadside food stalls were replaced by a wide-open grassland that smelled of sour cherries and sparkled with millions of plump dewdrops. Cocoa-barked trees with lacy, mushroom-shaped canopies reached skyward, reminding me so much of the Serengeti that I half expected to see a giraffe nibbling at the leaves. Rolling hillsides extended as far as the eye could see, each layer a more muted green than the last, until blending completely with the hazy horizon. Such startling beauty was impossible to enjoy, however, because the road was so rutted and potholed I was being spit about like popcorn.

We were bounced and jostled through a patch of dense rain forest down to a swollen, red brown river that looked impassable. But after a quick investigation, Wilfredo edged the SUV into the river and silent brown water eddied around the wheels. On the other side we barely had enough traction to ascend a steep, mud-slick bank with deep, squishy ruts. Slipping and sliding, we reached the top. I realized I'd been holding my breath and exhaled.

At first glance, Avellanas didn't seem all that special: a bald dirt parking lot, palm trees, blue water with an average-looking beach break, and sand as sharp as broken glass. But walking beyond the parking lot and glancing down the beach was like seeing in Technicolor after a lifetime of black and white. A stretch of salt-and-pepper sand curved gently north, overarched by wild jungle that dissolved into misty heights. Undulating fingers of shade drew me in to sit beneath the same kind of trees I'd seen everywhere—scraggly, with coffee-brown trunks layered with almond-shaped, bright green leaves. Dusky blue water swished up the beach, leaving curvy ribbons of white foam in its wake. And there were waves, waves, waves, and they were all empty. I stood speechless. Was this heaven?

On the way to the rivermouth, located about halfway down the beach, Flash identified an unnamed reef, which rarely worked during the rainy season, and Dead Tree, which he said was fun at high tide. At the end of the beach and farther outside was a heavy reef named Little Hawaii that only turned on during big swells.

While Kurt and Flash sized up the surf at the rivermouth, I stalled, noticing that the braided channel responsible for the wave flowed surprisingly clear. Multicolored sand grains tumbled and rolled in the current over miniscule ridges, their extensive journey from mountain to sea nearly complete. I looked upstream to the steamy jungle where the clouds had thickened, threatening rain.

I returned my attention to the ocean where Flash and Kurt were stroking into a lineup of steep and fast rights rising out of deep water. I waded in slowly, waiting for a lull before paddling hard to join them. I watched Flash, who surfed fast and aggressively, dropping in late and pumping down the line, exiting with flying leaps. He was so tall that he looked like a hunchback on his tiny board but his turns were fluid and powerful.

After sitting and watching for awhile, I caught my first wave, a pillowy, late drop—the turquoise wall forming a perfect curve in front of me. My heart pounded in my ears and my eyes flicked up, down, trying to memorize every detail. I raced down the line and was so enthralled that I neglected to chicken out and exit early like I usually do and as a result, the wave closed out on my head. Panicked, I thrashed and kicked for the surface only to find that I was standing in waist-high water, with sand in every possible crevice. I looked up to see Flash with his neck craned back to find me, a concerned look on his face. I shot him a smile that made him cock his head and grin before turning back to the horizon. I paddled out hungry for more waves but only worked up the nerve to catch one more before the ever-shifting tide robbed the wave of its punch and it was time to go. Warm rain pelted our wet heads and shoulders during the long walk back to the SUV. I couldn't wait to return.

After a delicious nap in our air-conditioned cocoon, Kurt and I were again headed for more surf. Playa Grande was just that—a huge, wide-open beach with soft brown sand. Grande is located along the same scoop of coastline as the camp but with a different aspect, so winds can be offshore when everywhere else is blown out. Same with the swell: when it's tiny in Tamarindo it can be overhead at Grande. A few of the surf guides, enjoying a day off, hitched a ride with us. I should have seen this as a bad sign, but I naïvely geared up to paddle out, even after hearing Augusto, one of the guides, describe Grande's A-frame wave as "very powerful," and tell me that the currents were often strong.

Strong was an understatement. Less than a minute into my paddle, arms burning with fatigue from my morning session, I was swept sideways down the beach as if I had jumped into a river. I made it back to shore and returned to where Augusto and the others had paddled out, scratching my head—they were almost to the lineup by then. How had they done it? I looked at the 7'4" funboard I'd borrowed from the camp. Flash had suggested I try it because Grande is too steep for longboards. I wondered if this new board was still too long, making it harder for me to cut through the current. I squinted to get a better look at the wave, and a feeling of unease crept into my gut. What I had thought was a head-high, crumbling wave was a thick-lipped monster exploding in the impact zone like mortar fire, with the occasional unlucky surfer getting obliterated by massive piles of white water. Hmmm, I thought. Time for plan B?

I spent the rest of the afternoon trying to teach myself how to duck-dive, a sexier, sleeker version of the longboarder's turtle-roll, where the surfer scoops herself and board beneath a breaking wave. It was tricky to get the board to submerge beneath me, it kept wobbling as my knee pushed it down, then it would shoot out sideways and I'd get tumbled in the massive pile of broken wave that I'd set out to avoid.

We returned to the camp, thoroughly spent, about an hour before sunset. Kurt and I bellied up to the bar for a cold one and then retired to the camp's tiny but perfectly warm beach-view pool. Halfway into feeling thoroughly relaxed and slightly buzzed, however, something happened. There were nice waves peeling along the beach. There were a few surfers catching some of those nice waves, with the setting sun casting a honey glow over the whole scene. The conversation went something like this:

Kurt: (long sip, big sigh) "Great day, huh?"

Me: (lying back, long sip) "Mmm."

Kurt: "My arms are worked." (sip)

Me: "Totally."

Kurt: (eyes following longboarder gliding serenely, jaw going slack) "Did you see that?"

Me: (climbing out of the pool) "Oh yeah."

Kurt: (drains beer) "Sunset session, anyone?"

I think I truly fell in love with surfing that evening. Maybe it was the low-lying sun filtering through the clouds, creating a painter's palette of purples, reds, and pinks against the blackening horizon; the forks of lightning flashing over the distant mountains; the dying afternoon wind leaving the ocean's surface smooth and glassy. Maybe it was the atmosphere: despite being super-crowded, the mood was playful. I recognized a few of the surf camp's instructors, all on longboards and managing to look graceful even as they were clowning around with tricks like headstands and goofy poses. People were cheering for each other, people were smiling. Or maybe it was that I caught one of my best rides ever—a left that I paddled for like I owned it, a fun drop that I had to call off a few surfers in order to keep, a long, backside ride that felt like flying and that made my heart soar.

That evening glass-off surf would become a tradition. No matter how tired, or hungry, or sunburnt we became, every day would end with a beer and a surf out front. Even at the end of our trip, after Kurt and I had sampled many of the area's beaches, shared countless waves, my best memories of Costa Rica were tied to evenings surfing that beach.

I was well on my way to surfing my brains out. On day three, Kurt and I surfed fun little close-outs in the pre-dawn stillness at a spot Abner had told us about. In order to get there, though, we had to paddle across a river, dodging the occasional bubbles from submerged crocodiles. "Don't worry about them," Abner said. "They're small." *Yeah,* I thought as I lily-dipped my arms through the water, *but they still have teeth!*

We had a blast, however, with the waves to ourselves and the sunrise a cotton-candy smear across a purplish sky. Then we made another discovery, a French bakery near the camp called Crocodillo. They served all the yummy French treats imaginable: airy croissants, *pain au chocolat*, delicious coffee, complete with lagoon-side seating where we could watch the crocodiles hiss and snap at each other.

Then we spent a double-session afternoon at Avellanas, sampling all the beach breaks and the rivermouth, catching fun little crash barrels, long peeling rights, and mellow high-tide rides. I spent my last hour surfing Dead Tree, going left and right, barely paddling to make the drop because the waves were so easy to catch. The sun dipped low and the water turned a smoky gray laced with ribbons of silver foam that pulsed over the roots of the scraggly trees on shore. Thunder rumbled from the pillowy black clouds hanging thick over the mountains. When Abner finally came to collect me, it was almost sunset and the water had transformed again—into a pale green, like frosted sea glass lit from within by the sinking sun.

My arms felt noodly from all the paddling and I was ravenous. My appetite had quadrupled—each time we headed back to Tamarindo for food, I ate like a mama bear coming out of hibernation. Surfing three sessions a day can do that to a person.

When day four dawned, I hadn't slept a wink because of

Sabana, a thundering beach break set in a deep-water bay surrounded by wild jungle. When I had drifted by the chalkboard the previous night to discover that we were headed there by boat, Augusto's normal mellow attitude and easy smile vanished. "Be carefuuul," he said, looking at me gravely with his brown-sugar eyes. "Sa-banna ees a heavy wave." He also warned me to *not*, under any circumstances, get caught inside, and to watch out for sharks because a family of them lived there.

*Oh great*, I thought.

We met our boat midmorning at a nondescript beach just outside of town and quickly hopped on. Beyond the muddy waters of Tamarindo the ocean became a deep, sapphire blue. Civilization disappeared in our wake and soon the coastline transformed into a dense and vibrant green, jam-packed with trees threaded by ribbons of mist. We passed entire schools of turtles and saw whale spouts on the horizon. Wearing faded Hawaiian-print board shorts and a shark-tooth necklace, our rugged Tico boat driver named Chilo rode the rolling swells like a surfer—grinning recklessly as he did off-the-lips and bottom turns while I gripped the gunnels. The rumored big swell had arrived as predicted. Our group of six guests plus Abner was palpably amped.

Except for me. I was scared out of my mind. I had decided to bring the 7'4" instead of my longboard—my theory being that 1) Sabana was a steep wave and so better for a shortboard; 2) if (heaven forbid) I *did* get caught inside, I would have less board to manage; and 3) if it became life or death and the only way back to the boat was to swim for it, I *might* feel slightly less remorse about abandoning a rental.

Chilo anchored the boat in the middle of a large bay edged by a pristine black sand beach overhung by clumps of spindly limbed trees. Fat lines of swell were stacked to the horizon and tossed the little boat stern to bow as they passed beneath us before continuing on, cresting and curling and erupting with dazzling spray. The wave was far inside of us and impossible to really evaluate. Deep blue ridges turned to frothy white piles of foam—they could have been two feet high or ten. I stared at the surroundings. Besides the wave, there was nothing there. No vacation houses, no parking lots, not a single other soul. It felt like we were on a stretch of undiscovered coastline, not a forty-five-minute boat ride from a budding resort town. Abner caught my stare and smiled dreamily. "Like old Costa Rica," he said.

The spell of admiration was broken when an approaching set hit an outer reef, crumbling like a demolished building before reforming into a smooth ridge of swell and steaming on toward the shore. Everyone on the boat froze, waiting to see that same set wave break against the beach. This watching and holding of breath in the presence of a set wave seems to be a ritual among surfers. I had seen it in Fiji, in Baja, even in the Northwest. Kurt had taught me to wait for a set before we decided whether or not to get in the water. "You can't really judge the surf until you've seen a set," he always told me. Set waves could come every fourth wave, tenth wave, only once every hour, but you always knew one when you saw it for its size and shape.

The wave peaked; I could see the deep blue lip reaching forward, then an explosion of spray sparkled in the sun like shards of colored glass. The wave then peeled perfectly for what seemed like an impossibly long time. The entire crew of surfers exhaled a simultaneous, "whhhhhhhhhhoa," before at once becoming a flurry of bodies rushing and jostling to get into the water. With a bemused smirk, Chilo underhanded our surfboards into the water like fistfuls of rice at a wedding. I smeared a final coat of sunscreen over my nose and dove in to retrieve my board. I was quivering with fear but what choice did I have but to surf?

Sitting in the lineup my throat was so tight I wondered if I might be having an asthma attack. *Do not get caught inside* rang in my head. I kept a constant eye on the horizon for the big sets and made sure to high-tail it for the outside when they arrived. *Do not get caught inside.* I watched Kurt, also on a shorter board than usual, paddle for a wave and get pitched over the falls, the wave exploding with a thunderous *boom* as he disappeared inside the massive foam ball. As much as I wanted to go in after him, to make sure he was okay, my brain had switched into self-preservation mode and all energies were focused on saving my own hide. *Do not get caught inside.* The next surfer paddled into a wave but with the same result as Kurt.

*Do not get caught inside. Breathe. Watch out for sets. Do not get caught inside.*

I paddled down the line a ways to get some perspective and to get myself out of the rotating lineup—I wasn't ready to drop in and get creamed while everybody watched. Another surfer dropped in and ducked beneath the lip, shooting down the line, the wave arcing in a perfect oval after him. An almost barrel. He carved a hard turn for the lip and flew over it just as the wave slammed shut in a thick mass of foamy, blue water. I followed his progress back to the lineup and saw that Kurt had made it back outside, too.

I noticed another wave breaking just off of the main peak. It was smaller and offered a shorter ride, but it was empty. I paddled over to get a feel for it. Even though less consistent, it didn't pitch out as forcefully as the main break. I decided to stay.

*Breathe. Do not get caught inside. Watch out for sets. Breathe. Do not get caught inside. Watch out for sets.*

After what seemed like an eternity, I spied my first wave and spun for it. Behind me, I heard the slight feathering sound the lip makes when it's starting to spill. When I dropped in and punched to my feet, I saw why I'd been warned about Sabana: the fat lip was folding at full-speed. I carved low around the breaking section, balancing against the alarming pace and steepness by grabbing my outside rail and crouching low, outrunning the pitching wall while my heart thumped like a base drum in my ears. The wave glittered a shiny, slate blue, thinning as it reached up. I held my breath and raced upward for the lip. *Do not get caught inside.* The wave pounded shut behind me, erupting with spray that peppered the backs of my legs like buckshot.

I paddled a safe distance outside and replayed what I had just accomplished. My mind relived the steep drop, my hand reaching for the outside rail (when had I learned to do that?), the fluttering, crushing lip folding behind me, my smooth, racing exit. I felt giddy. My first almost barrel. I couldn't wait to try it again. My next ride lasted a lifetime and left me breathless. And, to top it off, I did not get caught inside.

———————|———————

Dark clouds began to collect on the horizon behind us when out of the jungle another surfer appeared and paddled out. He was a Tico, small, shirtless, and riding a tiny board. Kurt had joined me by then, and we looked at each other with eyebrows raised as if to say, "What the heck?" Seeing no roads, I imagined that he was some kind of surf vagabond, hacking through the jungle to reach perfect surf, sleeping in trees, surviving on mangoes and bananas and the occasional roadkill. The three of us silently traded still-perfect waves for a short while until Abner signaled that it was time to go. With a look of remorse, Kurt spun on his board and said to the Tico, "It's all yours, buddy."

Suddenly, the Tico came to life. "You're *leaving?*" he said with only a slight accent before paddling into a wave and disappearing.

My eyes nearly popped out of my head. The vagabond spoke English?

The Tico returned. "Are you fuck-eeng *serious*, man? You're *leaving? Now?*"

"Yeah," Kurt replied, signaling to the boat, surprised too with this sudden communication. "We gotta go."

The Tico's eyes went half-mast and glassy. "So good righ now," he said, shaking his head. "So good!"

When he disappeared behind another wave, Kurt and I began our long paddle back to the boat, the Tico's words playing over and over in our heads.

The next day we returned to Sabana but this time by SUV. The long journey included a half hour on foot—first along a muddy, rutted road and then a faint trail along the beach. The moment we arrived it began raining and the accompanying stiff wind made a mess of the waves. It didn't even look like the same place. We discovered that a family operates a small campground there. Flash knew them, and since the waves were crap we walked to their makeshift cabin tucked into the jungle to say hello. To my further surprise, the lone Tico surfer we'd met yesterday, Alex, was there. Shortly thereafter, someone produced a bong and most of the camp got completely stoned.

While Kurt paddled out with Alex and Flash, I made love to the beach with my camera, burning through five rolls in an hour. The stormy surf and foamy shorepound contrasted perfectly with the overhanging scraggly trees and black sand. Later, Kurt chuckled as he told me about his session with Alex, who made the same "*so good* righ now," statement about the waves. "I wonder if he really knew how good it was yesterday, or if he's just always baked."

By Thursday, with near-blistered lips, bruises bigger than grapefruits, various cuts and scrapes, pulled muscles, and salt-crusted skin, my trip to the chalkboard began to lose its thrill. I was approaching surf saturation. Augusto could see it. "Maybe you should rest, take a day off," he said with sympathy. "No way," I replied, trying to keep my posture from giving away my weariness,

"I only have three days left!" I said, even though the idea of swaying the day away in a hammock was starting to sound pretty good.

Most mornings we would leave early, come back to town for a quick lunch, then depart shortly thereafter for another beach to catch a certain tide or evade the wind. Some days we were gone all day and we would eat typical food at lean-tos along the way. On the way back from Avellanas one time, Augusto introduced me to cassava chips, a snack that looked like a corndog without the stick, with mildly spiced meat inside a deep fried cassava-meal crust. The smiling lady behind the counter cut it open for me so I could doctor it with the local hot sauce. I began to crave cassava chips the minute the wheels of our SUV began rolling us home.

I did, however, take a little time out to plan a small birthday party for Kurt, contracting the Crocodillo to bake him a special cake and asking the surf camp's restaurant to make a few platters of appetizers for whoever wanted to join us. The creamy vanilla cake with buttery-sweet whipped cream frosting was gone two seconds after our guides and the instructors we'd come to treat as family finished singing "*Feliz cumpleaños a Kur-rrt.*" Soon everyone had a shot glass of tequila in front of them and we were toasting the waves, the jungle, and *pura vida.*

———————————+———————————

Just when it seemed like the trip couldn't get any better, we went to Witch's Rock and Ollies Point, two incredible waves located near the Nicaraguan border. After a crack-of-dawn start, we were once again on the road to meet another boat, this time in the tiny town of Playa del Coco. Kurt and I, along with two other guests plus Flash (joining us for fun on his day off), ate a nice breakfast at the edge of a powdery, cocoa-colored beach. Beyond, the tranquil, horseshoe bay lay still in the shadow of the high ridges to the east.

Walter, our seasoned boat captain, checked our passports and counted our cash before signaling for us to load up.

I had knots in my stomach from watching surf videos of Witch's Rock, known for its lightning-fast A-frames, howling offshore winds, and stories of an old, toothy crocodile living in the river that empties into the lineup. I was hoping that the second stop on our trip, Ollies Point, wouldn't be as scary. A right-hander that apparently breaks like a machine, Ollies is known for its super-long rides and forgiving nature. Armed with my trusty longboard, I had high hopes.

Walter threaded through a series of rocky islands, then raced along steep gray brown cliffs, until the last vacation home disappeared and we were surrounded by empty, barren wilderness. No people. No roads. We were on our own. The boat zipped straight across the wide-open, deep blue sea, its surface peaky with light chop.

Witch's Rock gets its name from the eerie fact that you can see it from everywhere. My first glimpse from many miles away was indeed haunting—a huge, square block of pale chalk seemed to glow with an otherworldly radiance. The name also comes from the shrieking winds that scream down the river valley and terminate just offshore. The rock itself sits in a wide bay and has little to do with the actual wave, which is a beach break cresting over sand bars created by the river.

Walter pulled the boat close and all eyes remained glued to the beach as deep-water swells lifted the boat and surged on toward the beach. I watched a razor-edged lip crest and then heard a crisp Zzzz-shhhhhhoooom as the wave broke. Someone said it looked small and was breaking too close to shore, but the offshore winds were light and the wave looked clean. Strangely, we were the only boat in the bay, a rarity at such a famous wave. One by one we plunged in.

It must have been the cold river emptying into the ocean at

Witch's, or maybe it was just my nerves, but the water gave me goose bumps. I rubbed them away while Flash surfed circles around all of us. He'd been keeping us entertained all morning with his goofy enthusiasm, and I suspected that he was still drunk from the previous night. We'd had to roust him from sleep that morning, Kurt pounding on the door of Flash's cement block of a room until finally he answered the door, disheveled and sweaty and smelling of the party he'd recently departed. During breakfast he'd told us with his typical heart-on-his-sleeve romanticism about the girl who was currently breaking his heart.

Witch's had seemed pretty tame on first look, but my first wave shot me down the line with lightning speed, the wind blowing my hair back. Arriving ridges of swell looked tiny but then jacked straight up, doubling in the time it took me to blink. I started to pay more attention, too, when I took a wave too far inside and after getting thrashed in white water thick with sand found myself in knee-deep water. "This place will break your board!" Kurt shouted to me over the constant barrage of exploding waves. I later wrote in my journal about Witch's: "easy to underestimate—don't!"

The wind kicked up, shearing the lips off the waves to blow shrapnel-like mist against my cheeks. It became difficult to see the drop while paddling into a wave, difficult to actually *catch* a wave. Increasingly, the wind shoved the nose of my board back into my face. When Walter called us back to the boat, I paddled in eagerly, anticipating better conditions at Ollies.

But my spirits sank like a stone when the large bay came into view, hosting almost a dozen anchored boats. "Must be why Witch's was empty," Kurt muttered, sighing. "Everybody came here instead." Walter and his assistant, a small, wiry youngster whose name I never learned (and who I will forever and to my discredit remember as "the cabin boy"), anchored the boat while I strained my eyes to get an impression of Ollies—how many people, how big was the wave, where were the lineup and paddle-out, were there rocks or boils—my mind grasping for any hint that the scene didn't look as bad as it did, but I counted at least forty surfers clustered together at the tight takeoff. I'm no good with crowds. My hope for grandeur shriveled up completely.

But we were there, so Kurt and I, along with one of the other guests and the cabin boy, grabbed our boards and hopped overboard. Flash was asleep in the stern before I'd even attached my leash.

Up until Ollies, I'd never really been vibed (in Fiji I think I'd simply been ignored). I'd heard of surfers giving other surfers the "stink-eye," intimidating newcomers or foreigners in the lineup by yelling things like "Go home, kook!" or by using aggressive tactics like dropping in on another surfer's wave, or just plain hogging all the waves for themselves. Some surf spots are so highly localized that the regulars who frequent the break warn others away by slashing tires, coating windshields with surf wax, or beating them up. It's rare, but it happens. Each wave is a one-time opportunity, and those who think they own that opportunity can get very protective. In a perfect world, surfers would take turns and let each enjoy their few seconds of fun. But it is not a perfect world.

The minute I paddled within striking distance of the lineup, the temperature plummeted, like a cloud covering the sun. Daggerlike stares met me at every turn, as if to say, "Who's the chick?" I tried being patient while watching three or four surfers fight for the same wave, kicking and stroking hard and yelling at each other until only one prevailed. But I didn't get any closer to the takeoff, which, being a point-break, is about the size of a futon. The scowling crowd was too thick and surfers returning from a wave would paddle inside of me instead of waiting their turn at the end of the line, effectively cutting me off. "Stay away" was their message, and I heard it loud and clear. So instead of sitting there, seething, I went back to the boat for my waterproof camera, traded my board for a set of fins, and stationed myself at the end of the wave so I could study it through the lens.

Turns out it was not such a bad trade-off. I witnessed countless beautiful waves—thin-lipped, almond-shaped barrels, sometimes with a skilled rider tucked tightly inside—and experienced none of the stress of trying to compete for them. I had a chance to soak in the view of pale cliffs rising above the beach, which reminded me of Baja with their cactus and prairielike grasses, and the shore cloaked in dark cobbles that shooshed and growled as the flux of foamy whitewash rolled them to and fro.

Eventually the crowd thinned and by the time I swam back for my board, only Walter's crew remained. And to top it off, the incoming tide had filled in the wave, making it mellow, more forgiving, perfect for a longboard. Perfect for me.

When I dream of surfing now, I dream of Ollies. I didn't just catch one or two perfect rides, I caught dozens and *dozens*. I'd paddle *one-two-three* and slide onto the soft, perfectly pitched slope, hopping to my feet to watch the pale blue wall rise up and extend into forever, my fingers raking the warm water at my side, my grin stretching my sunburnt cheeks. And I would fly, fly, fly, riding the wave until I began to wonder if in fact it had no end. When the ride faded, I aimed my body up and out, and as the lip crumbled into foam at my heels I would be prone, paddling with ease for the outside.

As the sun began to dip low on the horizon, the wave started pumping and I soon was winded and weary from the constant volley of paddle, ride, paddle, ride. Ours became that classic scene where friends shout "Take it, take it, man," to each other when a set comes in because everyone is too spent to paddle for it themselves. On my last wave, I lost count of how many turns I carved. My noodle arms could barely propel me back to the boat.

During the ride back to Playa del Coco, we were all silent, sun-fried, and completely surfed out, except for Flash, who, after his long nap and quick yet failed attempt at longboarding Ollies, was coming alive for another night of "party, party, party," and most likely, more heartbreak. "My frens," he cooed as we neared the shore, giving us the ubiquitous *pura vida* fist bump. "You are my friends."

Thank goodness for a roadside empanada stand during the drive back to Tamarindo or I would have buckled from starvation. That night, after barely having the energy to chew my shrimp and rice dinner, I collapsed into bed and slept until dawn.

I could have ignored my dawn patrol alarm the next morning. After all, it was our last day and our taxi would arrive by early afternoon to whisk us back to the airport. I could have spent a leisurely morning packing the surfboards, visiting the Crocodillo for one more *pain au chocolat*. But no, despite aches, pains, and peeling flesh, I, of course, went surfing and was treated to a solo morning glass on a rising swell. Kurt was still passed out cold when I returned, the windows frosty on the inside from the long night of air-conditioning. After showering I found him peering out the window at the surf, his face long. "I don't want to go home," he whined. Even though I had felt his guard dissolve somewhere around day two, and his "I'm here for the wife" torch disappear without a trace after one particularly sweet, late drop-in at Avellanas, it felt good to know that he'd fallen for Costa Rica, too.

Too soon we were packed and waiting for our ride. While Kurt took one last look for forgotten items in our room, I tried to find Flash and Abner. As if on cue, they breezed through the restaurant, shirtless and barefoot, with boards tucked beneath their arms on their way to the rivermouth, which, I noticed, was suddenly coming to life, firing with perfectly shaped peaks. Did I have time for just one more go-out? My arm muscles quivered with exhaustion and my skin was so fried from the equatorial sun that I barely recognized myself in the mirror. It was time to go.

I bumped fists with Abner and Flash, and wondered if they would even remember me in a week. I told Flash to stay alive until we could make our way back. "You're really coming back?" he asked, his blue eyes lighting up. I smiled and shrugged and told him that I hoped so. I thanked them for taking such good care of me, giving them a few bars of surf wax and what little *colones* I had left, and bid them "*Adios.*" They both smiled a knowing smile and gave me a quiet nod before heading down to the sand. Flash turned back and said, "Until next time, my friend."

# 7

# POSTCARDS FROM THE EDGE: BEAUTY AND SOLITUDE IN THE NORTHWEST

I COULDN'T HELP THINKING that we'd landed smack-dab in the middle of tropical perfection—just like in Timmy Turner's *Second Thoughts*, a film about three feral surfers scoring epic waves in Indonesia.

Long, peeling lefts, six-foot and glassy. No one out.

But we were not in Indo. We were shivering inside the van that Kurt had recently acquired, half-naked as we hurried into hooded five-millimeter wetsuits, booties, and gloves to brave forty-degree water, three inches of snow on the ground, and air temps in the twenties.

I couldn't have been more stoked.

We'd arrived beneath the cover of darkness the night before on the rumor of a big swell heading directly for our favorite haunts along the Northwest coastline. We had driven the van to California in search of surf, ditching the cold March skies of our home turf for greener, warmer pastures.

But California was flat. Nothing. No waves.

We'd waited a few days, resorting to checking a surf forecasting website. That's when we saw it: the perfect storm in the Aleutians spinning up a massive groundswell that would hit the Northwest in two days' time. We cross-referenced with the tide, local winds, swell direction, and stepped out of the Internet café breathless. Everything was set to line up perfectly.

"Whaddaya think?" Kurt asked, practically biting his nails.

I looked around at the miles of broad concrete sidewalks, glass buildings, and traffic-clogged freeways and thought of the hundreds of bodies I'd navigated to surf gutless ankle-biters the day before. "Head north, young man," I pronounced with a grin.

The place we both envisioned surfing peeled in front of an agate-pebble beach surrounded by old-growth forest. Conditions such as the ones predicted rarely lined up this beautifully. It just might be all-time.

Our longtime surf buddy Rick met us at the campground. Even though he was fully employed as a paramedic and the parent of two rascally, adolescent boys, he somehow managed to never miss a good swell. Team Creep—our adopted nickname, inspired by Rick's windowless, creepy van fit for a kidnapper—was the sole customer of the fifty-plus site complex, yet the winter caretaker gave us flak about trying to cook inside the group shelter. The crisp winter air and fat, wet snowflakes made cooking out in the open unappealing. We hid our six-pack of Black Butte Porter to avoid further trouble when the warden, a woman with a smoker's rasp and wild, black hair, drove down to check on us. "Lights out at eight o'clock," she barked.

The following morning we woke to a blanket of snow glowing beneath icy blue, clear skies. The campground offered no vantage of the break so there was no way of knowing if our thousand-mile gamble had paid off until we arrived at the beach. The snow had frozen to the roads, making our trip down to the coast arduously slow and dicey. We passed a big Ford pickup in the ditch, its passenger-side wheels still rotating in space, the loggers inside just emerging, shaken but okay.

We pulled up on scene, heater blasting. A few cars were parked, facing the beach—all strangely with Oregon plates—but nobody was about. Windows were frosted into an opaque white from the inside, signaling an all-night occupancy.

A broken wave was dying out close to shore. For a place that rarely offers anything to ride, just this fluff of whitewash held promise. Then a set hit, the lip teetering for an instant before crumbling, making a deliciously soft rumble that made my spine tingle with anticipation. The wave peeled forever, holding its shape.

I was out of the van like lightning, coffee cup in one hand, a fistful of my own hair in the other. "Whaa-hoo-hoo-hoo!" I cackled, hopping up and down and stirring the inhabitants of a beat-up Chevy Nova.

Another once-in-a-lifetime set began its slow, perfect crumble far on the outside. "What the hell are you still doing in BED?" I shrieked at the squinty face still wrapped like a mummy in a sleeping bag. Behind me I heard Kurt slide the van door open and I raced to join him.

Kurt, Rick, and I paddled out in the channel and beelined for the takeoff. Rick got the first wave and I remember the frizzling hiss of the lip curling forward, the erupting mist hovering in the windless air, the first rays of sunlight turning each droplet into golden prisms. I remember dropping into a wave in front of a mildly surprised Rick—it was a set wave, after all, something I normally shied away from. He looked on with a smirk as I dropped in backside and stood, relaxed and confident in the sweet spot, letting the energy of the wave guide me, grinning like a fool. I could have dipped low for a turn, I could have tried inching toward the nose, but I had found the Glide and the ephemeral moment seemed too fragile. I savored the glistening, lemony light coating the ocean's surface, the soft edges of the trees, the sound of spent waves combing the pebbly shore.

Even after my enthusiasm woke the sleeping interlopers, they still didn't paddle out for over an hour, well after the best sets had pulsed through.

———————+———————

"Adventure is not in the guidebook and beauty is not on the map. Seek and ye shall find." So say Terry and Renny Russell in their 1960s ode to the American West, *On the Loose*. But I'm sure Terry and Renny never went to the Trash Pile, the most unnerving, foul-smelling, and ugliest access point I have ever experienced. It's definitely not in any guidebook, though, and it certainly qualifies as an adventure just to find it, so they got that part right.

Areas of the Northwest are home to several Native American tribes, dry reservations that are heartbreakingly poor with a wild, unpredictable vibe. But the reservations also host pristine beaches complete with towering trees; sun-bleached piles of driftwood; powdery, dove-gray sand; and the occasional whale in the lineup.

Growing crowds and a need for breathing room had pushed us deeper into such territories in search of surf. On first look, the muddy gravel road we'd stumbled onto didn't appear to connect with the coast we sought. Team Creep crested a steep hill and I saw a towering, mishmashed pile of used appliances, broken toys, bald tires, all blended with acres of household trash. Our narrow road skirted the two-story-high mass and disappeared into a dark and woodsy dead end. We were really just looking to turn around somehow, and quick—get the heck outta there before a half-crazed local came after us with a shotgun. Then we saw it, a faint trail heading into a thick patch of alders. Maybe it was worth a look.

I stepped out of the van into a pile of dog crap and almost gagged at the stink of rotting garbage. We were quick to grab our boards and suits and head down the trail. I knew we were onto something good when we passed a disquieting bit of voodoo—a molding cloth doll with fraying yellow yarn hair and no eyes nailed through the head to a baby fir tree. The path was lined with salal shrubs, ferns, the occasional spiky devil's club, salmonberries, and a mixed canopy of alder, fir, and huge cedar. When I first heard the surf, filtering through the thicket, my heartbeat quickened.

Even without a pack on my back and a nine-foot longboard wedged beneath my arm, the hike would have been challenging: tight switchbacks; steep drop-offs; rocky, uneven footing slick with goopy mud. Wearing a wool hat, Gore-Tex coat, flannel-lined jeans, polypro socks, and rubber Wellies, I was drenched in sweat by the time we stepped onto the beach. The view, though, was worth it: brown-sugar sand pockmarked with gumdrop-shaped rocks edged by slivers of tidewater, sea-glass green water laced with bright-white foam. All a perfect backdrop for a gorgeous wave, if slightly sketchy due to some rocks and ominous-looking boils, but beyond, the open sea expanded into forever. It felt like the edge of the world.

Kurt looked at me and I looked at Rick and simultaneously, we all began laughing.

"Is this for real?" I asked.

Kurt had already turned his wetsuit right-side out. "I think we're in Hawaii," he said.

"Except for the cold water," I added, unpacking my suit and towel onto a drift log.

Rick's eyes twinkled. "Well, there's that," he said.

---

It was a beautiful autumn evening, the low sun melting like a butterscotch drop into a gauzy fog bank, the water a silky blue. In the midst of enjoying zippy little rollers, I heard "Shark!" shouted by a man surfing nearby. *Shark?* Adrenaline emptied into my bloodstream and in a nanosecond I was clawing toward the beach with images of teeth, blood, and pain cramming into my brain. I glanced sideways and saw Kurt and Rick paddling pell-mell for the beach, too.

Every surfer knows that sharks (aka "the landlord," "old toothy," or "the man in the gray suit") are out there, and that by swimming and frolicking in the ocean wearing black neoprene, we easily resemble their favorite snack, seals. But I'm usually too worried about staying alive in the actual *waves* to be gripped by the fear of a shark attack.

But the man who yelled shark had *seen* one. It probably had swum right under me!

I'll admit it: I've used sharks to my advantage to selfishly discourage people from surfing the pristine beaches along the Northwest's coast. Call it a form of crowd control. Yes, it's completely selfish and wrong on many levels—after all, great whites haven't been spotted here in decades—but when people say, "Wow, I dunno, *surfing* out there? Isn't the water cold? What about sharks?" my response is usually a shrug and a smile. If the cold and fear of sharks keeps them out of the water, who am I to stop them?

A slush pile of foam deposited me onto the sand and I ran, lurching my backside from the set of razor-sharp teeth certainly snapping shut behind me. My eyes probably looked as big as silver dollars when I joined the man and his son, still huffing and puffing and grateful to be alive.

With bulging eyes, the man told his story. "I saw at least four feet of back on that thing!" His son nodded gravely in agreement. Apparently, he'd seen it, too. "It was definitely a shark," the man sputtered.

Like Kurt, Rick also grew up surfing in California and looked skeptical. Kurt's face was neutral, but I could tell he was shaken.

The man continued. "I saw it swish its tail." He swam his hand through the air. "I saw its fin." All eyes shifted to the water, searching for a sign of the mysterious fin or a flash of its sleek, gray spine, or a dorsal fin caught in the light shining through the waves. But the ocean's surface was broken only by lines of approaching swell.

"Four feet of back," the man said again, showing us this time with arms spread wide. My heart was still pounding, but the man sounded a little less convinced. He coughed. "Or, it could have been a salmon . . . "

*What?* All heads snapped to the man. *A salmon?*

He kept his eyes on the horizon. "You know, they sometimes come up and swivel away like that?" He squinted at the sea and explained how he'd seen it before, surfing in Canada.

*Four feet of back on a goddamn salmon?* We grow 'em big in the Northwest, but four *feet?* Was this guy nuts?

"Um, *right,*" Rick said, his full-shine, BS-meter grin pegged. The man gathered his son and left. We watched them go, then turned back to the ocean, where the dying wind had left the black water shiny and smooth, each ridge of swell like a ripple of liquid bronze.

Unable to stomach the thought of the landlord lurking in the troughs of those peeling waves, I told the guys that I was done and left the beach. I figured they'd paddle back out but they followed shortly thereafter, claiming that despite the man's uncertainty, they were spooked. Soon, after trading our cold wetsuits for cozy cotton and fleece, we scrambled back to the beach, minty hot cocoas in hand, to watch the last of the sun melt into the sea. I thought I saw a pair of surfers in the lineup, waiting for their last ride, but it could have been the low light, it could have been my eyes, tired after squinting all afternoon looking for waves.

The next morning I woke early and scrambled to the beach for a surf check and found our perfect swell waning, with an onshore wind fresh against my cheek. *Dang it*, I thought. I spotted the man and his son down the shore, the man with a travel mug of coffee in his hands. He gave a smug nod. I went back to camp and wrestled into my frigid, damp wetsuit. Even though the conditions weren't nearly as good as yesterday, we had time for one more go-out before the long drive home, and since we knew it could be weeks or longer until our return, we were going to get wet. Kurt, Rick, and I had developed an unspoken credo: after driving four-plus hours to get to the surf, as long as the conditions were not death-defying, we surfed.

I navigated the soapy shorebreak and hopped on my board, gliding onto the gray green water and stroking hard for the lineup, the shark incident far from my thoughts.

I dropped into a wave and heard the rush of water moving beneath my feet, felt the elation of riding shotgun with Mother Ocean spread to my toes. I looked toward the beach and saw the dad and son loading their surfboards onto the roof of a shiny SUV. I kicked out of the wave and returned to the lineup, stealing glances at the pair. Why weren't they surfing today?

A splash broke the surface nearby, launching my heart into my throat. *Shark?* Frozen in fear, I gripped the rails of my board, watching the water beneath me for a sign, some indication that old toothy was back, that today was my day to meet the man in the gray suit. But there was nothing, and my heart slowed. I closed my eyes and told myself to relax. It was probably just a seal.

I thought back to the previous night when I had watched those clean sets spill in perfect lines against the shore, recalled the two people sitting in the lineup, enjoying pure sunset-session bliss, all to themselves, and I wondered.

I heard the SUV's engine turn over and snuck another look behind me. Did I see the dad toss me a knowing smirk as he drove away? My eyes narrowed.

There was no shark.

I'd been had.

Was this the cosmic Kahuna's idea of karmic payback? Intended to teach me not to be so selfish about sharing waves? Or was someone trying to beat me at my own silly game? Either way, there had definitely been no shark. I began to chuckle as I remembered the man's shark with "four feet of back." I remembered my eyes popping open, my arms working like windmills to deliver me to the beach. It must have been hard for the dad to not fall over laughing at my complete and total belief. Shaking my head, I dropped into another frothy wave and skimmed its bumpy surface for a split second before it closed out. I came up grinning, my fear gone, my ocean safe again.

"Sharks? Nah, we don't have 'em up here," I could picture myself saying the next time someone asked about old toothy. "The real danger, though," I'll add, leaning in for effect, my arms opening wide to demonstrate, "are the giant-sized, man-eating salmon, from Canada."

———————+———————

One winter morning, Kurt, Rick, and I paddled out in semi-messy, short-period boomers after a heavy sea-storm in the night had rearranged the beach logs. Pulverized bits of seaweed suspended like a cloud in the water made for resin-colored, murky waves that were making me slightly seasick. And I was cold. My feet were cold. My hands were cold. My face was cold. I studied the misty horizon, the black-rock seastacks, the high cliffs crowded with green, century-old trees. I shivered in my thick wetsuit, and paddled over to Kurt. "Let's move to Mexico," I said.

He looked at me and smiled. "Soon," he replied.

During a trip the previous fall, as the campfire glowed and the turbulent surf pounded the shore, Rick made another round of mojitos and our normally tame conversations about work and family slipped a notch into the dangerous territory of Things We Still Wanted to Do with Our Lives. It started with Rick describing a recent trip to Mexico and how easy it would be to start a business there. Then I shared the story of a friend who'd just returned from Baja. A local offered her the surf-front property she'd had to herself one morning in exchange for her '93 Subaru. I postulated out loud to Team Creep how much land we'd surely get for my truck. Then Kurt pitched the idea of starting a restaurant (he was a ski-bumming chef in his former life), and just like that our warm-water-surf-hungry minds had melded into one solid dream machine.

"That sounds like one wild ass plan," said Rick. "Maybe I'd even get Kitty to buy into it."

Rick's wife, Kitty, keeps us in line—she's our Voice of Reason. However, the three of us know that secretly, she has Wild Ass Plans (we've started calling them WAPs for short) of her own, like buying a horse and razing her backyard to make a perfect pasture.

"She could ride her horse on the beach," I said.

"Well," Rick said with a chuckle. "We'd have to buy her a horse first."

We stared into the crackling fire, thinking on that a minute.

"Aren't you writing a novel?" Rick asked.

I sighed. "I am." Truth was, I had written two, but it seemed nobody wanted to buy them. My travel-writing career, as well, was turning out to be more of a hobby. My yoga/surf retreat story had not even garnered a response from *Yoga Journal*, and after dozens of other queries I had settled for a sterilized two-pager in a low-circulation yoga publication out of South Florida.

"She's gonna make millions," Kurt said with a grin, stirring the coals with a stick.

"Well, hey," Rick said. "There's our funding."

"Right." I rolled my eyes. "Okay," I said, playing along. "I solemnly pledge my first million for WAP funding."

Rick's eyebrows arched.

Kurt shrugged. "Sounds like a plan to me."

Over the next few days, our list of WAPs grew to ridiculous lengths. Rick wanted to organize a paddle board race across Puget Sound. Kurt wanted to convert our van to run on biodiesel. Rick wanted to shape surfboards in his garage. Kurt was itching to build a cabin somewhere. Besides yearning to surf every possible corner of the globe, I was dying to clear my slate of all the piecemeal side jobs I had been doing since quitting my teaching job, so that I could write full time. I justified it to the guys as a way to more quickly acquire that first million.

So when Kurt's reply to my Mexico question was "soon," he was only partly lying. "Soon" had become a typical WAP response that meant, "Yes, as soon as we get funding clearance, which could be any day, we'll do it."

Looking at the frozen sky and waiting for waves, I crossed my arms and put my gloved hands in my armpits, hoping for warmth. Kurt spun and dropped into a thick wedge of an amber brown wave. I turned to Rick, whose lips were pinched tight from the cold. "Have you sold that novel yet?" he asked. I sighted an incoming wave and spun for it. "Not yet." I replied, smiling. "Soon, though," I added as I began paddling. "Definitely soon."

———————+———————

The van crept down the windy road, pausing ever so slightly at the vantage point over a set of houses.

"Crap!" I said, eyeing the dishwater gray waves at the river-mouth below.

"Might just be the tide," Kurt said. "Let's check it anyway."

Because my spotty, ever-shifting work schedule and Kurt's days off were so random, we were able to surf midweek when crowds were thin. But that didn't always translate into good conditions. Waves break 360 days a year on the Northwest coasts, but wildcard factors like wind, tide, and swell direction make trip planning a challenge.

The narrow parking strip was empty, a sure sign of nothing to surf. I followed Kurt along the muddy path, our dogs, OJ and Sophie, darting in and out of puddles, frisky after the long drive. I felt certain that we should press on, maybe hope to find something sheltered from the wind.

The day wore on and the beaches passed by in a blur: an exposed point too messy, a rivermouth flat and windy, a cove breaking big and right on shore. We knew checking our favorite spots would be pointless and anything facing west would be taking the brunt of the strong winds. With hope held high in my chest, I climbed a tree a few feet to look down on a hidden point that can often be tucked enough out of the wind to produce decent rides. But all I could see through the thicket of alder branches was blue green froth. We considered the drive to La Push but knew it would be blown out, too.

"It could have been six feet and glassy," Rick said with a sigh. "It just wasn't."

We were skunked.

Out of options, Rick pulled out his flask containing the amber liquid he affectionately refers to as "surf enhancer" (or nap enhancer, depending on how bad things get) and soon we were suiting up beneath leaden skies for the short paddle across a murky river to a wide bay offering short-period, thumpy close-outs.

Sometimes you just need to get in the water.

---

The first time I went to Short Sands in northern Oregon, I went for the waves. The second time, I went for the coffee. And the Mexican food, and the gourmet natural-food munchies at the Co-Op, and the hot showers at the campground, where Kurt repeatedly fell asleep in front of the campfire.

The van door slammed shut and I wrapped Sophie's leash around my wrist and told her to stay close as I walked toward the path leading down to the beach. *Yeah, right*. Sophie was off like a rocket, with me straining to keep up. I had forgotten her pinch collar—a major oversight as she is the strongest sixty-pound lab on planet Earth. I understood her excitement, though—we were finally out of the stuffy van, with the search for surf (or in her case, freedom to roam) nearly complete.

I tightened my hold around Sophie's leash and the Drifter, my recently acquired longboard that rode so well it seemed specially made for me, and made my way down the graveled forest path. Stopping once for a breather, I heard a trickling creek and glanced into a narrow clay-walled canyon. Faint scents of iron and pine mixed with the thick sea air.

Overhanging boughs of scruffy fir and cedar framed my first view of the water: a shiny, deep blue with little bumps of swell and black-clad surfers bobbing in clusters. The view opened further to reveal an immense, square-shaped bay set deep inside high, rocky cliffs topped with virgin forest. I followed the railroad-tie staircase to a wide swath of smooth, bowling-ball-sized cobbles and strained to control Sophie, who had spotted the water. I saw other dogs running loose across the wide beach, and so I let her go. Behind me, Kurt did the same with OJ, who trotted after Sophie.

We found a vacant drift log up on the berm of cobbles and set up shop: towels, board bags, water bottles, sunscreen, a few meager snacks. The waves looked fun, a little crowded, which always makes me a bit anxious, but clean and mellow. Perfect summertime surf.

Sophie begged me to play fetch, so I tossed the ball into the water a few times, trying to wear her out. When we headed out into the surf, OJ drifted off toward the north end of the beach, tracing some irresistible scent. Later, he circled back to our stash of possessions to faithfully await our return. Sophie hovered at the water's edge, hitting up every emerging surfer for a quick toss of the ball. Desperate, she sometimes swam out to us in the lineup, her legs kicking hard and strong, her breath wheezing from the freezing-cold water, and I had to paddle her in before she tried to scrabble on top of my board and clawed me to pieces in her panic.

Many of the surfers in the lineup lacked experience. The realization that I was not one of them filled me with satisfaction. After sitting in countless lineups, waiting, watching other surfers drop in with confidence, *I had arrived*. I wondered if Fiji was finally paying off. Even though my skills had not progressed there, it had certainly elevated my fear threshold, giving me a kind of boost in small, easy surf. I was tempted to take more than my share of the waves, but I wasn't so far removed from being a beginner that I had forgotten the frustration of being out-maneuvered. After a while, I snuck off to a corner where I enjoyed a nice little right all by myself. The tide was moving in quickly and the waves got bigger and more groomed. I found myself not getting scared, but eager. I remembered something Louise, the Baja Surf Sister instructor at the yoga camp, said to me. "I used to see set waves and get nervous. Now I get excited." I wondered if such a transition could be happening to me.

The sun sunk low, lengthening the cold shadows. Kurt and I took our last waves in, changed, gathered the pups, and migrated to Manzanita, the nearest town. We cruised the main street and found Left Coast, a fresh Mexican food place with a sunny deck and cold *cervezas*. The evening air held a bit of a chill, perfect for getting cozy in a fleece hoodie. As I waited for my dinner, I leaned back in the plastic chairs, letting the last rays of the sun heat my cheeks, my muscles at peace after such a mellow, fun evening session. Up north on the Rez, the only fresh guacamole and chile-lime chicken tacos were the kind we made on a campstove.

Originally, we had planned to explore more of the area on this trip, but the combined ease of access, dog-friendly beach (in California, even leashed dogs aren't allowed near the sand), and fun waves in a beautiful setting had sucked us in. So after enjoying the remains of a driftwood fire on the beach, our eyes on the black, star-studded sky, and the dogs limp from exhaustion at our sides, we decided to stay.

That night the constant hum of waves caressing the coast soothed us into delicious sleep. We woke to a thick coating of dew. "No campstove, *please*," I moaned, dreading the setup of the fickle contraption, the wait for boiling water, the tedium of brewing via single-cup filter held in my cold hands. "Surely there's got to be a decent Americano in this town?"

Kurt rolled over, smacking his lips after such a good rest. No one had come banging on our door during the night to check our user permit, no one had been dealing crack from the rattle-trap motorhome on stilts at the end of the beach, no fireworks had shocked us and the dogs awake at 2:00 AM. "Hmm," he said, scratching OJ behind the ears. "Looks like someone here's gone a little soft."

"Can you blame me?" I asked, snuggling back into my bag. "This place is cush."

We didn't have to search far for coffee, and the barista made me an Americano ten times better than any national chain (big surprise, but it was even better than Kurt's). I savored every last drop, all the way to the parking lot, another summerfun day at Shorty's in my sights.

# 8

## COSTA RICA REVISITED

"HONEY, IS EVERYTHING OKAY with you and Kurt?" my mother asked me over a plate of calamari.

"Yeah," I replied, giving her a confused look. "Why?" Kurt and I were going back to Costa Rica, this time with our entire posse: Rick, my surf-girl buddy Leah, and Rick's friend and neighbor Steve.

She sighed. "It's just that, well, all these trips you're taking. . . ." She trailed off, looking away.

My mom certainly had reason for concern. In the last eighteen months I'd quit my teaching job, spent my savings on a laptop and several warm-water surf trips, and only gotten out of bed before eight o'clock in the morning if there was something to surf. I guess the idea of us heading back to Costa Rica was a red flag.

"I just want to make sure you're not running away from something," my mom continued, her eyes boring into me with such desperate concern I started sweating.

"Just the cold water," I said, reaching for her hand.

---

The superheated air rising off the black tarmac filled my lungs like a rescue breath given to a drowning victim. I drank in the moment, savoring the humidity, the honey-scented breeze, the distant mountains veiled by black-capped thunderclouds.

Witch's Rock sent two vans because our group was so large and because we had so many boards: two large hard-case coffins containing Kurt's, Rick's, and my longboards; Steve's soft case with a mixture of long and short boards; plus Leah's short board. We had arrived in mid-May, at the end of the dry season. Although every day the clouds thickened and the gestating humidity peaked, it had not rained since the previous November and it showed: the countryside was a blanched, dead brown, peppered by the occasional parched tree, their canopies thin and droopy. Yet the ocean was a serene, turquoise blue, and the roads were dry, smooth, and soup-free. After a winter of thick wetsuits, arctic winds, frozen sand, and choppy, wedgy waves, the afternoon paddle-out in front of the resort with my friends felt like pure glory. Even the fiery-hot sand burning my feet couldn't dampen my desire. The swell was pumping and rumored to peak at six to eight feet in the next day or so. Winds were offshore and perfectly light. I saw faces I remembered from our last trip—those who had sung *feliz cumpleaños* to Kurt and who had surfed side by side with us during our sunset sessions. They waved, their eyes lighting up with surprise and welcome. I didn't see Abner until the next day, but Flash was waiting for us at the front desk when we returned from the surf, brimming with stoke.

"My frens," he said, practically glowing as he bumped fists with Kurt before grabbing me in his arms for a huge hug. "That's my girl," he said shyly, nodding at the board. He must have seen us out there, seen how my surfing had improved. I beamed at him, feeling proud of myself. We had little time for a proper reunion, however, because a small welcome party was revving up in the bar. Before I gave in to the festivities, I snuck a look at the trusty chalkboard. Our group's week of tours would start at Avellanas by boat with Chilo, followed by an afternoon at Playa Grande, also by boat, with a guide named Ricardo. I sashayed into the bar to share the good news.

———————————|———————————

"What's the wave like?" Leah called out to me from behind her bed as she rustled through her suitcase. "Is it gonna be big?"

"Probably," I answered, as a knot of nervousness tightened my gut. "The swell was never this big last time," I added.

"Dude," Leah said, pulling on her sun hat and smearing sunscreen across her nose while looking in the mirror. "I'm so gonna get worked."

We clambered onto the boat right in front of the resort, then lickety-split Chilo, wearing his same old rakish grin, opened the throttle. I felt like a rock star with such streamlined service, and I could tell that my friends were impressed. It felt good. I wanted them to love this place the way I did.

But when Avellanas's broad, speckled beach came into view, my spirits fell. The empty perfection I remembered from our trip before was replaced by a California nightmare: crowds as far as the eye could see. Chilo pulled the boat to a deep anchor between the rivermouth and the Little Hawaii reef Flash had pointed out to us last time, which was empty. I watched a few sets roll in but couldn't really discern the wave's size or power. Besides, I was practically in a frenzy to get in the water—my brain fueled by the memories of all the fun waves I'd scored during my last trip. I was over the gunnels and paddling for Little Hawaii before most of the group had located their rashguards.

But if ever there had been a time to sit back and take stock, to really assess the conditions, it would have been that first day back at Avellanas. The swell was at least overhead, and there was nothing gentle or forgiving about Little Hawaii. I huddled in the ever-shifting lineup, trying to keep my place despite the massive amounts of water moving around. Steve was the first to catch a wave and disappeared behind a gigantic peak. I scanned the back of his wave as it swept toward shore, but he remained hidden.

With a mounting sense of dread, I turned back to the horizon only to see Kurt paddling out toward the largest wave I had ever seen. I flung myself onto my board and began paddling deep, hard strokes for the outside. Ahead of me Kurt paddled up the face, the teetering lip a luminous, frosty green. My breath moved in time with my screaming biceps: *left, right, left, right* as my eyes remained glued to that lip. Up, up I went, shooting for the bright blue sky. Suddenly I was launched over, just as the lip cracked, crunching down behind me, exploding in a terrorizing *boom!* with spray that stung like buckshot.

I steered toward where Kurt and Steve huddled together, expecting them to be just as intimidated as me and ready to try somewhere else. But to my dismay, just as I arrived Kurt spun and paddled into the first wave of a set; Steve followed on the next while I paddled like hell to the outside to avoid getting crushed. Once safely out of harm's way, I scanned the area for the rest of our crew and was surprised to find Rick walking down the beach. Leah, who with her shorter board had paddled farther inside to wait for waves, suddenly appeared on shore as well, inspecting her board. I frowned. Had something happened? Why was Rick walking away? And I hadn't seen Kurt return yet, was he okay?

Steve had found a new takeoff, way deep, and was catching wave after wave. Finally, I caught sight of Kurt. He too, was walking down the beach. What the . . . ? I squinted south, toward the rivermouth but all I could see were black specks. I watched Steve for awhile, the walls of water easily dwarfing him, rising high above his head and sending big frothy piles of white water after him. Ribbons of brown-tinged foam and microscopic bits of flotsam coated the surface of the water all around me, a sign of big energy. I suddenly felt very small. And alone.

I made it to the rivermouth after a long but mind-clearing paddle. Kurt relayed his story about getting spanked at Little Hawaii after the wave he'd caught walled up and nearly crushed him as it closed out. I waited a while to assess the crowd of long- and short-boarders mixed together, elbowing each other for waves, before finally claiming my first. I will forever remember the long, smooth drop, landing squarely toe-side, my eyes sighting down the perfect crescent of pale blue water. This was *better* than I remembered. Halfway down the line a shortboarder seemed on the brink of dropping in on me but saw that I was on my feet and cooking fast down the line and pulled up. I was relieved, and thrilled because I wanted to ride that wave forever.

When I hopped off in the shallows, Rick was there, waiting for a lull to paddle back out. I was grinning from ear to ear and expected Rick to be smiling huge, too. After all, the water was warm, the waves were good, we were on vacation, right? But his brow was wrinkled in concern.

"You okay?" I shouted over the pounding surf.

"Yeah," he replied, squinting. "Got a chunk taken outta my board."

"What?" I said, keeping one eye on incoming waves. We both saw the lull and hopped on our boards to paddle out.

He shook his head. "Leah ditched her board."

I gasped. I could still hear Karen's, "Never ditch your board," in my head. Surely my friend wouldn't do such a thing? But I never got the chance to ask for details because Rick and I separated then as we usually did—Rick likes to sit deeper and moves around a lot in the lineup. It's probably the reason why he seems to get the most waves. That and the fact that he's not shy about occasionally snaking me and Kurt, but we let him—he's kind of the alpha in our little group of three.

Leah would later swear to me that she had not ditched her board. She had been paddling back out at Little Hawaii and hadn't even seen Rick behind her when a big set bowled her over. They got rolled up together, their boards colliding somewhere in the mix. Thankfully no one was hurt.

I could sense trouble brewing but didn't let the drama faze me because I was hungry for waves. Something in me had changed since my first paddle out there. I was more confident, more at ease with the waves, more willing to take risks. It was a good feeling, and I spent that first morning enjoying every second of it.

After the tide shifted, our group clambered onto the boat and headed back to Tamarindo. Spending three hours beneath piercing, dry-season sun had drained us. Rick, whose pale Irish complexion had turned a strawberry pink, set off to buy a surf hat and find someone to fix his board. Leah was able to patch the small ding in her board with session-saver putty. The rest of us ordered lunch in the camp's restaurant, cooling the lingering tension with a few beers. By the time two o'clock came around, the only surfers in our group still excited about getting back on a boat were Leah and Steve. Plus, Kurt and I knew that with such a big swell, Playa Grande would be death-defying on longboards, so the two of us plus Rick decided to surf out front.

———————————|———————————

After it was just the three of us, someone ordered shots of tequila and soon we were on our way to the beach break half-lit. Rick borrowed one of the camp's 10'2" single fin longboards—a complete log, and after a few endlessly long rides, I began to see his smile return. Even though the waves were big for the beach break, they were manageable, and a lot of the beginners that normally infiltrated the lineup were absent, so I didn't have to navigate an obstacle course of bodies when I rode a wave to the inside.

Rick was having so much fun that Kurt trotted back to the camp and traded his board for the camp's other 10'2". Pretty soon they were dropping in on everything: set waves, leftovers, close-outs, they even shared waves, hooting and laughing. People began noticing them and started joining in on the fun, or at least staying out of their way. The sun dipped low, casting a coppery sheen across the darkening water. Surf lessons ended and the Tico instructors came out to play and soon the evening session magic was back, just as if we'd never left.

That night our group reconvened in the camp's bar to compare notes. Wild-haired Ricardo, easily the shortest and possibly the youngest Tico surf guide at the camp, had already downed half his beer—eager to get out on the evening prowl—and nodded toward Leah. "Sheez crazy," he said in what I would come to know as his typical understated style. Apparently Leah, whose tough-as-nails mentality I had experienced many times before, had dropped in on countless double-overhead monsters at Grande, landing a few but mostly getting thumped. I imagined being her: going over the falls again and again and again, choking on seawater, getting wrapped up in my leash or cut by my own fin, the massive momentum of water ripping at my limbs. *One* of those wipeouts would have been enough for me. Not Leah. They had been there for *hours*. I turned to her in amazement and she shrugged. "I keep thinking that if I keep going for it, one of these times it'll work."

We made the short but steamy-hot walk across town to Pedro's, a simple seafood restaurant with unbeatable prices. Even though it was already dark, I was shocked at the changes in Tamarindo. No longer the simple surf depot with muddy streets—it now hosted a Burger King, a late-night espresso bar, and newly paved roads crawling with gringos. I lamented only a moment on these "upgrades," so focused was my brain on the next day's waves.

After an early breakfast of store-bought cookies and instant coffee, our group was jumping off the boat at La Tortuga, a huge beach near a tiny town of the same name. La Tortuga has the unique setup of having no offshore reefs or islands to dampen incoming swell, which is another way of saying that the waves at La Tortuga are always bigger than anywhere else.

I had felt sure that we would be sent again to Avellanas that day because there were so many choices there for our mixed group, and with such a big, rapidly increasing swell, going to a place like La Tortuga seemed sketchy. But Abner described the waves as big (liked by shortboarders) yet pillowy (great for longboards). Plus there were plenty of peaks all along the beach, so we could spread out. *Perfect*, I thought.

And it was. Fat lines of swell materialized on the horizon and lumbered into the bay, forming the friendliest big waves I have ever surfed. I was petrified on my first ride, dropping in with my heart thumping in my ears, the lip arching up so high I had to lift my head to take it all in. But the wave set up nice and easy, and I soared down the line. The lip even feathered, sending little tufts of spray tumbling down the slope, and still the wave didn't break. As the ride began to fade I arced a steady curve upward and slid over the lip, giddy with delight. I paddled back to the loose lineup, where Kurt, Steve, and I were gathering, to do it again.

After a while of trading waves, the swell seemed to increase by the minute. Directly in my line of sight was the abandoned boat (apparently, Chilo surfed), increasingly being yanked end to end as the massive swells passed beneath it. When a huge outside set nearly broke on top of the boat, quick as lightning Chilo was back onboard, relocating it to safety. I began to get nervous.

At some point during all of this, I irked Steve. Before the trip we were strangers, so I treated him as an equal and assumed he would do the same for me. But at La Tortuga that day, he kept paddling inside of me at the takeoff. I let it go because I'd rather eat my own toenails than be confrontational. One time, however, I'd had enough of his unfair positioning and so pivoted for an incoming set because it was my turn. Apparently Steve thought otherwise, because the minute he went for the same wave and saw me ready to drop in, his exasperated look said volumes about the pecking order he'd constructed in his mind. We both pulled up and he paddled off in a huff. He kept his distance from me after that, both in and out of the water. I was frustrated—what gave him the right to steal waves from me, then treat me like an outsider when I didn't jump out of his way?

Then I lost track of Kurt. He had taken a wave and either was still on his way out or had moved on to somewhere else down the beach. Turns out he had gotten caught inside, and while he toiled away at paddling and getting worked in the towering piles of whitewash, I too began a paddling marathon just to keep from getting creamed. Set after set loomed on the horizon. I paddled out farther and farther but the sets kept coming, some breaking on top of me. I started to panic as my turtle roll no longer worked and every wave picked me up and slammed me into the depths. La Tortuga had seemed so innocent; this sudden violence had caught me off guard.

I had spent months preparing for the physical demands of this trip, with hours and hours of laps at the pool, extra sit-ups, and as many surf sessions as I could arrange. Even so, my arms were becoming limp with fatigue. I wondered if I was in some kind of funky current that kept me from the outside—why were there so many breaking waves? I started to get really scared when after getting thrashed by an incoming wave I had to actually swim *up* to reach the surface. That's when I said to hell with Karen's rule and ditched my board. I paddled up the next wave and when it began to break I pushed my board away and dove beneath the folding lip, my leash tugging hard at my ankle. I surfaced, quickly mounted my board, then paddled up the next wave and ditched again. I wasn't thinking about how it might look. I wasn't thinking about Karen. Every muscle was tuned to getting me back outside. Slowly I made headway. I didn't stop paddling until I reached the boat.

Sitting there on my board, bobbing up and down with the king-sized swells, letting the fear and panic drain out of me, I shook off shaky tears. I tried to tell myself that getting rattled like that was a good reminder that Mother Ocean calls the shots. But I was disappointed in myself. I had panicked and kooked out. I was no better than the girl I'd scolded on the beach the night before— the one who told me her board had "slipped," even though I'd seen her let go of it in the whitewash. It had nearly smacked me in the head. "Never ditch your board," I'd told her.

Kurt appeared shortly thereafter, nauseous from the seasick-ness that comes from battling big rollers and completely spent from his long paddle. "I'm done," he told me, his eyes pinched and his cheeks green. "Get me outta here." Fortunately the others, beaten down by the relentless sun and demanding conditions, were on their way back to the boat. Leah, a medical student and the daughter of two physicians, carried a stocked first-aid kit and had something to help Kurt. He fell asleep in my lap halfway through the trip home and slept well into the night.

———————|———————

The morning we left early for Witch's and Ollies, we were late for our pickup because I had to doctor up a hole in Kurt's side— a paddle abrasion gone bad. Steve started calling me the "night nurse," after the Gregory Isaacs reggae song, because I seemed to be the nursemaid for everything from cut feet to indigestion, or an ear for their venting of so-and-so's behavior or who was doing what to whom. I hoped the nickname meant Steve didn't still hold a grudge against me and so I smiled whenever he and Rick would sing, "Night Nur-r-rse . . . the pain . . . is get-ting worse." But by the time our day at Witch's Rock and Ollies Point came along— something I had been looking forward to since the day I'd left—the building drama within our group weighed heavily on my shoulders. Couldn't we all just get along? I was ready for a break from the conflicts, and for that day I decided to put it out of my mind.

———————+———————

Walter pulled up alongside the massive, chalky-yellow rock at Witch's Rock, and despite the big swell and light offshore winds, the waves were empty. I wondered if that meant Ollies Point would be crowded later, so I tried to focus on enjoying the rifling rights at Witch's. Our group splintered off into our own spaces, which I thought was just as well—it seemed like we might explode if frictions increased. I tried not to feel disappointed—I had pictured our happy camp of surf buddies sitting in the lineup, trading waves, laughing, egging each other on, etc. It may just have been our differences in approach: Leah rode a shortboard and liked to charge hard; Rick was the stylist and chose his waves carefully and did not tolerate anyone in his way (e.g., shortboarders sitting inside); Steve was the wildcard—he had brought both types of boards and sometimes he surfed solo and sometimes he picked off peelers next to us longboarders. Kurt always placed the needs of the group over the needs of the individual, which was at odds with individuals wanting to do their own thing. And we were all eager for waves, including me. For such a group to surf in harmony was impossible.

I watched Rick drop into his first wave and disappear behind a screaming-fast right, then Kurt took off. Spray was erupting all over the place, showering us with fine, salty mist. I missed my first two waves, probably because I was too scared to wait at the deeper, more accurate takeoff. I crept inside a little, waited my turn a few more sets. Finally, I shook out my fingers and narrowed my eyes on an incoming wave.

I spun and paddled and the next thing I knew my board had become a rocket ship. I sprang to my feet, the wind tickling the tiny hairs on my cheeks, my ears buzzing with the sound of the wave breaking behind me. The wave sparkled a deep blue but I could see the shore fast approaching, the lip curling forward. I had no way out so I straightened my board toward the beach. With a menacing *boom!* the wave closed out on my heels, shooting me straight to the sand. I hopped off in the fizzling cloud of white water, then turned around to paddle back out, struggling through beatings from incoming waves but finally making it outside, breathing hard and feeling shaky. I managed one good ride that didn't close out on my head before Walter's signal to circle the wagons.

To my bewilderment and relief, Ollies was not crowded; just a handful of boats greeted us as we entered the bay. I couldn't figure out why—when I paddled up to the wave, it, too, was exactly the way I remembered it, the same forgiving, perfectly peeling right I had been pining for since the minute I had turned my back on it. I settled into the lineup and watched for a while, getting a feel for the other surfers already there, letting the energy of the wave soak into me. It felt good to already have the place dialed. It seemed like a part of me had been missing all these months and at that moment, I was complete again.

After my first wave, when everything fell into place again and I was soaring, gliding, flying forever, I was in the Zone. Everything around me fell away—my friends, the other surfers sitting in the lineup, the beautiful surroundings. There was just me, my board, the wave, and my smile. Wave after wave after wave.

I suppose I should have noticed Leah's frustration. I suppose I should have noticed Steve waiting way out on the outside for the rare big set. But I didn't. Or if I did, I didn't care. If ever there was a perfect match between board, rider, and wave, it was Ollies, me, and my nine-foot Drifter. For the rest of the week, every other stop on our tour didn't matter to me. My friends and the world of other surfers could have all the waves they wanted. But not Ollies. Ollies was mine.

Then I heard Kurt's shout: "It's my fuckin' wave, Ratcliff!" Yanked from my own private world, I watched Kurt in a paddle-battle with Rick, who pulled up and let Kurt have the wave. Kurt dropped in and stood up, his head passing beneath me. But then he fell, and Rick howled with laughter. Kurt returned half-mad, half-laughing, but something was amiss. After that, I backed down a bit and let waves pass, waves that I wanted so badly and that I knew I could ride. And when those waves went by unridden—either missed or flubbed by the surfer who claimed it —I felt a deep, visceral ache. Surely, I deserved to hog this wave just a *little*? Surely, after setting up the trip in the first place, for being good-natured through all of the drama, I could be granted a few hours of bad behavior?

I sensed that I'd pushed the limits of the surfer's code with my greediness, but every muscle in my body was singing with joy when finally I clambered onto the boat—the last one on—and we started the long trip back. I was still giddy when we steamrolled into the camp's bar for our nightly pre-dinner round of beers and "nachos as big as your ass."

"I'm buying tonight," I proclaimed, grinning.

"So you can make up for dropping in on us?" Steve said, an edge to his voice.

My smile slipped a notch. My mind replayed the afternoon at Ollies. Had I really dropped in on my friends? I may have been wave hungry, but nothing in my slide show of images from the day showed me cutting anybody off or sneakily paddling inside the others at the takeoff. "I let lots of waves go by," I replied.

"Leah didn't get one wave out there to herself," Steve continued.

I wondered why Steve wasn't also angry at Rick, who, as usual, rode the most waves that day. Who'd snaked waves from *me*, from *Kurt*. Why was I the only one who was supposed to play nice? Wasn't it all of our jobs to take care of each other?

Rick eyed Leah and shrugged. "It was a longboard wave," he said, igniting the tension between them again.

Leah looked away and I remembered seeing her sitting on the inside of us longboarders, kicking and thrashing hard to get into a wave, and I knew it had been wrong of me to hog the waves the way I had. I had been selfish and unfair.

"I tried to get everybody to form a lineup," Kurt said, ever the peacemaker. "But nobody would listen." He grinned at Rick. "That's why I had to call Rick off."

"And then you ate shit," Rick said, laughing.

Kurt laughed, too, and I could feel the tension ease.

"I'm sorry," I said to the group and I meant it. But I could tell that my hopes of our group coming together were dashed. The damage was done.

———————+———————

"There is no way I'm getting in a boat today," Rick said with glazed eyes as we walked to breakfast the next morning. He'd woken with a sun blister on his lower lip, his freckled skin practically glowing and his finicky spine tweaked after the bumpy ride on the boat the day before.

"The board says La Tortuga," I said. "By boat."

Rick closed his eyes.

"Why don't we see if they'll take us by car?" Kurt said.

———————+———————

An hour later we were pulling away from the camp in an SUV with boards of all sizes stacked to the sky. Ricardo had arrived to accompany us, shirtless and wearing huge white-rimmed sunglasses. "Let's go Sabana," he said without breaking a smile. As if he'd snapped his fingers, our driver pulled onto the road. The rest of us shrugged—what did we know?

After bearing the steamy humidity and cramped quarters for nearly an hour, we wove through jungle down to the beach and parked beneath a grove of palms. The group clambered to the shore and I chased after them with my camera. But when I got a view of the bay, I stood in awe, jaw dropping at the sapphire blue water, the black crescent of sand, and the top-to-bottom barrels firing all along the beach.

"Ho-ly crap," said Leah.

Ricardo, ever the Mr. Cool, actually looked excited, a tiny smile tugging at the corners of his full lips.

I followed a surfer with my eyes as he paddled in and sped down the line of a grinding barrel while the lip curled over him, partly obstructing him from view until he came careening out to fly over the lip. It was the kind of thing I'd seen in surf videos, never in person.

Paddling out on a longboard would have been suicidal. If we had wanted to surf in such conditions, we should have arrived by boat, like the time Kurt and I had been there before. Even then, however, a longboard would have been dicey. These were overhead barrels at a heavy beach break. Despite Ricardo's enthusiasm to surf, in the end we decided to move on and spent the next three hours failing to even get to La Tortuga—a flooded river blocked our route—before returning to the camp.

Rick and Kurt promptly threw back a shot of tequila each at the camp's bar, then stormed the beach break with the 10'2"s. Leah and I joined them and the day ended with another magical evening session, the air ringing with lots of laughter and, "It's my fuckin wave, Ratcliff!" even though there were plenty of waves to go around.

We spent our entire final day at Avellanas (by car), overruling

Ricardo's "Let's go Sabana" decree the minute we got in the SUV. On the way he suggested we hire him as our personal surf guide next time we came. "We could get a boat, head up the coast, whatever, man. Email me. It's rastacostarica at hotmail dot com." He slid his rock star glasses back up, his expression still of a half-bored celebrity. "I was gonna have it be 'rastacostaricapuravida' but that was too long."

"Ya think?" Rick asked with his trademark sarcasm.

Somehow the crowds were elsewhere and the remaining visitors were spread evenly along the beach. We surfed all the breaks (except Little Hawaii, which without the big swell wasn't even working), sampled the beachside restaurant's smoothies, ceviche, and shady hammocks. We convinced Leah to try a longboard and after she'd caught her umpteenth wave, said, "This is awesome! Why didn't you guys tell me about this before?" Rick only rolled his eyes. I tried to savor every wave, every sigh of contentment, every scent of the sea mixed with sunscreen and surf wax. I knew it might be a long time before I returned—possibly never. And even if I did return, would it be the same?

Kurt and I had the chance to surf one of the many little beach breaks together, just the two of us, something we somehow hadn't been able to do yet. There was nobody else around. The waves weren't perfect like at Ollies, but it didn't matter, it was a little lime green slice of heaven. I'd paddle *one-two* and drop in and feel Kurt's eyes follow me down the line. I'd paddle back out and watch Kurt paddle *one-two* and smile at me and hoot with delight as he went left or right. We volleyed like that for the rest of the session, laughing at all the silly little sayings that surface during a trip with so many characters, talking between sets about how much we would miss it there, how much fun it was to share it, to see its beauty through someone else's eyes.

"So good right now," I cooed.

Kurt tossed his head back and laughed. "So good!"

# 9

# YES, VIRGINIA, THERE REALLY ARE WAVES IN SICILY

"I THINK I'M GOING TO GET offered a job in Sicily tonight," Kurt said as he pulled our van onto the deck of the Port Townsend ferry. "Are you still in?" he asked while a man in an orange reflective vest slid chocks beneath our wheels.

We had talked about it ad nauseam but it still thrilled me to think we might actually move across the globe for two years. Friends and family members had practically swooned: The wine! The food! The cappuccinos! "Such an opportunity!" they said. "You'll have the time of your lives!" And, if it wasn't love at first sight: "You can do anything for two years."

"There's surf there, right?" I asked.

"That's the rumor," Kurt replied, reaching over the longboards spooning in the back to grab our jackets.

"Then I'm in."

Once at our camping spot, we made sure Kurt's cell phone had service before snuggling beneath quilts and sleeping bags inside our van, near enough to the winter waves that they practically lapped beneath the chassis. The phone rang just as I was drifting off to sleep.

"Mr. Waeschle," the woman's voice said. "We would like to

offer you a three-year contract for the position of . . . " I didn't hear
the rest because my mind had stopped at the three years part.

Kurt's eyes widened. He'd heard it, too. "Excuse me, but did
you just say *three* years?"

There was a brief pause. "Yes, is that a problem?"

Kurt covered the receiver and looked at me, slightly panicked.

I cringed. Three years sounded like a long time, but in terms
of Kurt's career, this was a whopper of a WAP. Plus, I would be
able to write full-time, just like I'd always wanted. I sighed and
shrugged. "Let's do it," I said.

"I accept," Kurt said into the phone.

If mainland Italy were a boot, Sicily would be its soccer ball,
surrounded by the Mediterranean. I'd read about winds blowing
over Africa and producing good surf on the south coast, winter
storms born in the North Atlantic that swept over Spain and
whipped up swells that stormed Sicily's northern shores. Supposedly waves even broke on beaches within thirty minutes of where
we hoped to live. I'd seen pictures on a Sicily surf website of pretty
green waves and surfers riding them.

I was blissfully unaware of my peril.

For the first few weeks, we were high from the newness of it
all; of buying bread baked in a wood-fired oven, of drinking the
ultra-strong *caffè*, of the sweet fragrance emanating from the miles
and miles of orange groves, of experimenting with the sing-song
language. Sophie and OJ had survived the long travel but were still
wary, sidestepping the empty kennels and panicking every time we
had to leave them. We scoured every possible location and finally
found a rental house near the edge of a rocky scoop of coastline
edged by high cliffs, a short drive from a small fishing village. We figured that we might never again get the chance to live on the ocean,
so it might as well be in Sicily, on the government's dime.

Kurt loved his job as the chief of a small fire station operated by the U.S. Navy and staffed with Italians. His crew made him pasta lunches and *caffès* and tried to teach him Italian. On weekends we explored the rocky flanks of the very active Mount Etna or some of the possibly surfable beaches I'd read about. We drank coffee or ate *limone* granitas and the dogs romped on the empty, waveless beaches.

Months went by and the surfboards stayed in their weatherbeaten travel bags, unridden. Our mountain bikes and hiking boots also were not getting any use. Early on, we'd hiked to a lake that allegedly held the "highest naturalistic value in all of Sicily," but which turned out to be a murky duck pond complete with carp. It was so gross I didn't even let Sophie swim in it. Apparently the people of Sicily are too busy baking bread, harvesting oranges, and drinking coffee to recreate. Land was valued for its ability to produce food or host edible animals.

I grew anxious. Had we made a mistake in coming here?

Then it got hot. 100 degrees, 105, 117. I'm a Northwestern girl through and through—to me a hot summer day is anything over eighty degrees. Soon we stopped going out on excursions. Our car's air-conditioning could only do so much. When I began waking up at 6:00 AM with temperatures already topping ninety degrees, I started to unravel.

As the late-August afternoon heat soared, cooking my brain, I called Kurt. "Can we go home?" I pleaded.

"It'll get better," he said.

"It's so hot," I blubbered. "And everything's dead and dried up."

"I know," Kurt said. "I miss home, too."

I flopped into a heap on the cold tile floor and closed my eyes as the oscillating fan blew hot air over my face. I thought of surfing fun little peelers at Short Sands, of the cool pine forest trails we always mountain biked when the waves were flat, of the majestic, snowy Cascade Mountains, and cried.

—————|————

"Good news," Kurt said after greeting me at the door one after-noon in early September. "I met a guy who surfs here."

My eyes lit up for the first time in weeks. "Really?"

"And he says there's a swell coming."

My heart leapt. "When?"

"Saturday."

When the day came, we loaded the boards onto the roof of our recently acquired two-door Alfa Romeo hatchback (practically an SUV in those parts). As we pulled onto the *autostrada*, people shot us strange looks. Apparently, the people of Sicily don't ride longboards.

Kurt turned onto a gravel road beneath a white arch that read, "Lido de Capinine." Like everywhere else in Sicily, we had to pay a wrinkled-up old man a euro to park even though the lot was empty. I followed Kurt along a crumbling cement wall adorned with graffiti to an open section of beach, a stiff wind cooling my cheek. Empty lawn chairs, umbrellas, vacant wood platforms with tentlike tops lined either side of the expansive coastline. There was even a bar, several in fact, albeit boarded up, spaced evenly along the beach.

The wave, if one could call it such, was a small, wind-blown, choppy, short-period nightmare. With shoulders slumped, I watched a black-clad shortboarder, one of three in the water, try to pull an air off of a collapsing peak and fall.

"It's not that bad," Kurt said, sensing my lack of enthusiasm.

I raised an eyebrow at him.

"Come on," he said, putting his arm around my shoulder and steering me back to the car. "Let's at least get wet."

—————|————

I was still waking up every day wanting to bolt when Agnone Bagni gave me a reason to stay.

"Another swell's coming," Kurt said when he called to say hi in the middle of his twenty-four-hour shift.

I clicked my tongue. "Let me guess. Capinine is gonna be firing."

He chuckled. "I guess everything is gonna be firing."

I raised my eyebrows. "Well then I guess we don't want to miss the swell of the century, do we?"

"I love you," Kurt said.

"I love you, too," I replied.

---

Kurt's surfing source, a guy named Steve, called late the night before the big swell to say that the buoys were still indicating good, clean waves. We agreed to meet at Agnone Bagni (pronounced an-Yon-ay bahn-Yee), a straight strip of sandy beach just north of our little cove that had been packed shoulder to shoulder with beachgoers just a month before.

Every now and then, lines of swell would push into the bay fronting our rental house. The northern point had a shallow, reefy rock ridge that compressed the swell into waves, but they broke right on that reef. Kurt had even tried to surf it once but had scraped his fin on the rock, nearly separating it from his board, and landed in a bed of spiny, black sea urchins. We gave up hope of surfing out our front door after that.

The morning dawned and we could hear waves combing the shore inside our bay, which we took as a good sign. Boards were loaded and coffee mugs filled and in less than twenty minutes we were on the road.

Steve called from Capinine and said that it looked good there, so we passed Agnone for a chance to check it out. But messy Capinine just looked bigger than usual, and with gnarly currents.

"It's probably just morning sickness," Steve said, readjusting his visor to peer out past the shorebreak. "It'll probably get better."

The three of us stood watching thick-lipped close-outs pulse toward shore. Despite the completely uninviting setup, I was game to surf. I thought I might snap unless I caught a wave soon.

"We could check Agnone," Steve said. "It might be better there."

I groaned. "Whatever we do, let's do it soon."

"Let's go Sabana," Kurt said with a grin, channeling Ricardo.

"On the road again," I said with a sigh.

---

There are many beautiful beaches along Sicily's coast, but Agnone is not one of them. The stretch of dirty sand slopes steeply into blue, semi-murky water that turns the color of mud when it rains. There is trash everywhere: on the beach, in the water, blowing down the dusty road.

But, by God, there were waves.

Ripples swept into the bay in neat, curved lines for as far as the eye could see. Line after line after line. I watched a set stretch skyward, then pitch and crumble, growling as it peeled the entire length of the sand bar. Shoulder-to-head high. Glassy. No one out.

"I don't know about you," I wheezed, feeling as electric as a live wire, "but I'm going surfing."

As I paddled out, a hazy, mist-drenched fog moved in, jacking up the humidity and making the horizon one with the water. I heard waves approaching before I could actually see them. The faint glow of sun turned the water a pale, opaque green, like scuffed sea glass.

As in every first wave in a new place, I dropped in with all senses alert: Was it powerful? Mellow? Punchy? Would the inside section knock me on my keister? I was pleasantly surprised to find it was mellow and gentle, a little like Short Sands, and long enough for me to walk to the nose a bit, like at La Push. The water was still warm from the summer sun so my choice of trunks and a two-mil wetsuit top was perfect.

I stroked back outside, practically wiggling with joy.

"You needed that, huh," Kurt said.

"Yes I did," I replied before spinning around to drop in on another wave.

We surfed until the swell died out about four hours later. We emerged happy, tired, and hungry. Just like old times.

———————+———————

Slowly, we got the hang of forecasting Sicily's short-fetch surf. In contrast to the Northwest, where we often knew about an approaching swell for as much as a week, Sicily's surf could come up in a matter of hours. And unlike the Northwest, Sicily had far less consistency, with most of the good swells arriving in the fall months; winters were sometimes big but mostly too disorganized to surf; springs were windy; summers were flat. It wasn't ideal, but at least I wouldn't die of wave starvation.

We met a few other Americans, all attached in one way or another to the base where Kurt worked, who also surfed and who composed almost a club: besides Steve, a shortboarder, there was Rich, a lifelong longboarder, and Scott, a Hawaiian who rode anything. Often the five of us were the only ones in the water.

One time I was surfing Agnone alone after a big November storm. The surf was mellow and the sun bright. Suddenly I heard the blades of an approaching chopper and watched it skim the shoreline no more than a few hundred feet above the water. They came right for me and when they passed over, I could see the men's attention focused on me. They swung back around and I had to squint to keep the rotor-wash mist out of my eyes. Suddenly I wondered if they thought I was a shipwreck victim, stranded from shore by the waves, floated by some shattered piece of the wheelhouse instead of a surfboard. Either that or they were just stunned to see a woman out of the kitchen or not doing her husband's laundry. I wasn't sure how to wave them off so I just smiled and sat there trying to convey tranquility. Finally they buzzed off.

Another time, when a freak summer swell hit the southern shore, Kurt and Steve paddled out at a popular swimming beach. They practically parted the crowd parked elbow-to-elbow on the hot sand but when they began paddling past the swimmers, the lifeguard blared his whistle. When Kurt and Steve didn't paddle in, he got out his bullhorn and shouted incomprehensible Italian warnings in between whistle blasts. After pacing the shore for a good ten minutes—righteous enough to yell but not serious enough to enter the water himself—he finally went back to his tower. If the crazy Americans wanted to drown in the scary surf (it was maybe chest-high), so be it.

When the Italians did join us in the water, it was rarely before eleven o'clock in the morning. Apparently, Sicilians don't dawn patrol. They also don't know about the fierce "locals only" mentality present almost everywhere else in the world. I had read travel stories about surfers visiting some strip of coastline and stumbling upon not only great waves but locals who knew nothing about surfing. The surfer would describe their first paddle out, when the villagers would emerge from their huts to watch the outsiders brave the big waves. After a few days of this, the little kids would be out playing in the leftovers, riding planks of plywood or anything else they could find or nothing—spontaneously figuring out how to bodysurf. Everybody would play and laugh and share. Nobody fought over waves, nobody paddled inside, nobody hogged the lineup, nobody scowled or called anybody off or sat stoic and unfriendly. It was just play. How magical to experience such purity.

Sicily is no forgotten corner of the world, but its residents have remained sheltered from surfing's dark, aggressive side. Maybe it's because surfing is such a fringe activity, or maybe it's because the wave-to-surfer ratio is high—the maximum number of surfers in the lineup, including myself, never topped ten. Or maybe it's because big-name professional surfers have never traveled to Sicily, bringing aggression and territorialism with them the way the Pilgrims brought smallpox. It certainly isn't that Italians are inherently nicer surfers—in Costa Rica I'd surfed with packs of them, enduring their constant banter, their intimidating shouts intended to keep me from dropping into waves.

Another time I was surfing Agnone with a few of our friends. The swell was waning and I was thinking of paddling in when a tiny car showed up and four young men emptied onto the sand. I watched them smoke cigarettes and strip down to their teeny Speedos before wiggling their skinny frames into full wetsuits despite the bathlike water temperature. They paddled out right into the breaker zone—apparently unaware that there was a channel—got completely worked by a series of waves, and emerged still talking nonstop. Finally outside, they smiled and said, "*Buon giorno.*" They cheered for each of us when we caught a wave. They laughed at themselves when they paddled and missed. They could have dominated the peaks with aggressive body language and posturing (watch one of these young males behind the wheel of a BMW and you would see that they certainly have the skills to do so), and you could argue that they had the right. After all, we Americans were the visitors. But I hoped for their sake that their little golden age of surfing would outlast us and the many Americans yet to come.

In the meantime, three years started to feel like not nearly long enough.

# 10

# BIG WAVE SEASON IN MOROCCO, THE COME SEE! STATE

THE RED TAILLIGHTS OF OUR TAXI disappeared into the desert night as Kurt and I, weary from the long travel, each hoisted our longboards and luggage and shuffled into a cramped, pitch-black hallway. Sounds of feathery waves caressing a shore we couldn't see funneled upward, as if we stood at the back of a deep cave. Kurt found a light switch and we descended carefully past piss puddles and trash—the tips and tails of our boards scraping the dirty, tiled walls around each corner—to what we hoped was the correct door. After a tentative knock, Kurt stepped back to wait.

"Nice place," I mumbled to Kurt, half asleep against the wall.

Kurt yawned. "I'm just glad our boards made it."

I agreed. The Sicilian airline agent, a slender young woman in a tight pencil skirt and heels and with the most beautiful mane of thick dark hair I'd ever seen hadn't known what to do with our longboards. "Suurif boarde?" she asked in stiff English, her frowning eyes skimming a computer screen. Not finding what she was looking for, she pursed her pretty lips. "Mmm. I don theenk so," she said before instructing us to wait. She then disappeared and my blood pressure began to climb. Finally she returned. "I must charge you ten euro extra per kilo," she said. Relieved at the board's admittance but dreading the tariff—even *one* euro per kilo would be more than we paid in the States, I expected her to direct me to a scale somewhere, but she asked instead, "How many kilos?"

I didn't miss a beat—after so many exhausting dealings with airline agents who always hassled me about the size, the length, the weight of my longboard, and made me pay extra and waive any rights I had to expecting its safe arrival, this was my one chance to even the score. "Twenty," I said even though it was probably much closer to forty, or the equivalent of ninety pounds. "*Va bene*," she said. But after calculating the whopping price, she shook her head. "I theenk it too much," she said, and suggested fifty euros. Ah, Sicily, the land of the flexible.

---

The apartment door opened and Rick's bleary, freckled face poked out. "Hey!" he said, grabbing Kurt's board and yanking him inside, then coming back for me. "Surf Sister!" he bellowed as he hugged me tight. "Welcome to Africa!"

Team Creep, together again.

We'd rented our two-bedroom flat through Surf Maroc, a pseudo surf camp in Taghazout, Morocco, was really more like a *one* bedroom plus a thinly padded bench along the living room wall. The bathroom was a one-stop shop, tiled to the ceiling with a shower head in one corner, a drain in the middle of the floor, and the sink and toilet close by so you could technically take care of all your bathroom needs in one go.

But oh, the view: our balcony overlooked the expansive Atlantic, where rollers crested and swished across a checkerboard-patterned rock-slab coastline, creating a soundtrack better than any stereo. The buildings along the cliffy coast all had the same advantageous setup: floors were constructed above street level as well as below, hence the reason we had descended to our room the night before but were still two flights up from the shore. Our patio had outdoor cooking facilities, plus a table and chairs. Over cups of instant coffee doused with dollops of canned, condensed milk early the next morning, Rick and Kurt, who'd been separated for almost a year, shared the latest work, family, and life adventures, the crisp morning air ringing with our laughter.

Then it was time to surf. Rick had arrived the day before and recommended Tamri Bay, where he'd found some fun rides. I was a little confused. We'd come to Morocco for the reeling, peeling points, not some lowbrow beach break.

"I checked all the points on the way up there," Rick told us, reading my mind. "Nothing." But a big swell was on the way. Things would get interesting soon enough.

"Well let's *vamanos* then," Kurt said, downing his coffee.

"You mean *allons-y*," I corrected in my best nasally French accent, happy to finally put my one foreign language to use.

Up the four flights of stairs we went, tilting our longboards up and down to get around the tight corners and sidestepping the same piss and trash from the previous night, winded by the time we broke into daylight.

We crossed the dusty street to a silver Renault Berlingo, a compact cross between a minivan and a jeep that was part of our rental package, and loaded the boards. Pale, desolate hillsides dotted with green scrub rolled upward from the cliffy coastline as we steered north. The crisp cerulean Atlantic stood out in sharp contrast to the sparse, dusty desert, its refreshing wetness pulling at my already-parched cells.

We were waved through a police checkpoint, the guards wearing neatly pressed, army-green uniforms and scowls, then another farther up the road. It was a little nerve-wracking, being Americans among Muslims during a tense time in world affairs. We passed open bays and high, rocky points, home to prickly trees

and shrubs with dainty white flowers. Waves were breaking everywhere, but the bays were too small and closing out right on shore,
the points dangerously close to the cliffs. For all the hype about
Morocco's perfect surf, things were looking bleak.

"Watch out for the gypsy kids," Rick said as we pulled onto
a makeshift gravel parking lot high up on a bluff. We'd left all of
our valuables behind as per Rick's suggestion, and it was obvious
why: three groups of hawkers made their way toward us. A guy in
faded, wrinkled clothing wanted payment for parking, a pair of
persistent boys with bright-white smiles wanted to sell us t-shirts,
and a man in surf trunks smoking a hand-rolled cigarette said he
could find us the best hash this side of Amsterdam. We ignored all
of them, saying, "No, *merci*," and walked to the edge of the cliff to
assess the surf.

Massive, beautiful-blue, wide-open Tamri Bay glistened in the
midmorning sun. Big, frothy-lipped waves curled and crumbled
in front of a sparkly caramel-colored sand beach. Bobbing surfers
huddled in loose clusters: three here, a handful there, a pair of
body boarders playing in the whitewash, a small group heading
out for lessons. It didn't take us long to suit up and scramble down
the steep trail to the water's edge. I eyed the head-high sets and
hoped I still remembered how to handle waves like that.

For sure, I was a bit wobbly on my first wave, my heart beating fast and my breath high and tight in my chest. I dropped in
backside, the satiny wall of water rolling, thinning, folding at my
heels as I raced for the shoulder. I paddled quickly for the outside
after flying over the lip, while the panic ebbed and the joy seeped
into its place.

Rick and Kurt were farther down the beach, lost in calls
of "It's my fuckin wave, Ratcliff!" and asking which one of them
brought the 10'2"s complete with emergency tequila dispensers.
On my second wave I made sure to savor the smooth glide of my

Drifter sailing down the line, the offshore breeze buzzing past my ears, the trickling whisper of my fin cutting through the seamless slope of water. After a while the waves started getting bigger and the tide came in fast. Paddle-spent and hungry, the three of us agreed that it was time to hunt down breakfast.

To my delight I was able to read the French menu at La Bas, the outdoor café just down the street from our apartment back in Taghazout. In the daylight the little town reminded me of a dusty Old West outpost, except the surf mecca/French roots/Muslim business upstart version: dark-eyed men in long, hooded robes discussing business in the open square, rich young Spaniards toting surfboards, and fresh baguettes being delivered to the cafés via rickety bicycle. A handful of businesses and restaurants lined the street—most of them catering to surfers: a nightclub-like restaurant overlooking the water, a tiny surf shop, two hodgepodge groceries, an Internet café, and a t-shirt shop.

Rick ordered a round of mint tea, the local brew that our waiter, Rachid (also the owner), hailed as "Moroccan whiskey." Each tarnished, beat-up pot arrived individually, steeped to perfection with enough added sugar to produce hyperactivity. But the toasted-rice-flavored green tea soaked with a fistful of fresh mint, stems and all, was the perfect beverage for the arid, dusty setting. It was even poured *à la française*, the waiter standing erect with one hand bent at the small of his back, pouring a delicate stream while lifting the pot high, still pouring into the tiny cylinder of a glass until nearly full, then finishing with an elegant flick of the wrist and a curt nod.

We toasted to our new adventure just as the midmorning call to prayer rang from the town's loudspeaker. It felt strange to just sit while Muslims prostrated themselves on tiny carpets, chanting their prayers, but soon it was over and the streets were bustling again. I ordered a Moroccan omelet, which had sweet peppers, tomatoes, mouth-watering spices, and a mild, creamy cheese made fresh that morning, all served in a small black skillet. And because I couldn't resist, I had to try their café au lait. It was rich and delicious and could have been airlifted from some posh *rive gauche* eatery. We left stuffed, food- coffee- tea-buzzed and only a few dirhams lighter. Morocco began to grow on me.

———————|———————

That afternoon we loaded boards onto the Berlingo and set out to find the most longboard-friendly point, unimaginatively called Bananas (pronounced bin-*nonn*-ahs by the blonde British surfer girls at Surf Maroc HQ) after the nearby Banana Village, whose main income was the sale of, naturally, bananas. We found the village (and the rows and rows of bananas), which also had a functioning bank and a cute little *patissierie*, complete with croissants, chocolates, and fruity, cream-filled tarts.

After weaving through a neighborhood composed of shacks, barefoot children playing with sticks in the dirt, and men loitering on the corners, the road dead-ended on a broad plain of sand far from the distant point and its waves. We thought about proceeding on foot when, out of nowhere, a man riding a camel approached. He was dressed head-to-toe in thin layers of white and pale blue fabric, his head adorned with a royal blue turban, the wide tail of it hanging like a boyish lock of unkempt hair. A whip the length of his thigh dangled from his fingertips. I dug out my camera to capture this fine example of desert life—figuring he was on his way to the next village or some distant oasis to trade silk or figs or whatever. The camel came closer, seemed to be heading right at us, actually. I snapped a photo and the rider barked some command to his camel and was on the ground in seconds. He bowed with a kind of ta-da curtsey and beckoned me closer.

"No, *merci*," I said, waving him off. I didn't want to delay this man from his long journey.

"Come see," he insisted.

A camel driver who spoke English? I should have known then what he was up to. I stepped back. "No, no," I said again. "*Merci beaucoup.*"

Rick and Kurt had been squinting at the waves, muttering phrases like "afternoon wind" and "small swell" and "nothing to ride" but began watching me closely.

The driver motioned that he would take my picture sitting on the camel. I tried to resist again but he seemed dead set on connecting me with his trusty steed. "No," he insisted. "Come see!" Finally I relented and climbed into the wide, padded saddle. I figured I'd sit for a quick pose and we'd be done with it. But the driver suddenly called out and the beast rocked forward, his back legs extending and nearly knocking me head-first into the sand. "No!" I cried out. Then his front legs went vertical and I was whipped backward, my grip on the saddle's metal handles the only thing saving me from a backward somersault. "Get me off this thing!" I shouted. But the camel driver only smiled blithely.

Kurt and Rick were chuckling as I pleaded for the man to let me down. I thought about jumping but I was up so high I figured the impact would probably break both my legs. Then we were walking.

"No!" I shouted again, beginning to panic. "*S'il vous plait!*"

"How's the wave look from up there?" Rick asked with a smirk as the camel picked up speed.

"Shut up!" I shouted.

I babbled on, trying my French, commanding him to release me. Finally, through my thick skull I realized he was no wandering pilgrim, he was a salesman. "*Je n'ai pas de l'argent,*" I said. I don't have any money. Which stopped him in his tracks. His dopey smile faded and the light went out of his eyes. Without speaking he turned the camel around. I was ready for the camel's hard, jerky descent to the earth that time and hung on.

The driver gave me back my camera but did not leave. We really didn't have any money on us (for security reasons), but I dug through the back of the Berlingo anyway. I wondered what would happen if I failed to produce. Would he demand my watch or my backpack as payment? Would he get his camel to spit on me?

I came up with two travel-squished Luna Bars, one a lemon-zest flavor and the other a chocolaty peppermint stick—my personal favorite. I shrugged sheepishly and held them out in my hand, hoping it was enough. He squinted at me. *"Pour vos enfants,"* I said, improvising. For your children. To my relief, he nodded in seriousness, as if this was a fair deal, and tucked the bars into a fold of his robes. Then he led the camel up the road, the two of them plodding onward in search of more lucrative prey.

The next day brought a cold wind from the sea and a marked increase in swell size. On our way out to check the waves, we were accosted by Mohammed, a fisherman who always seemed to be waiting for us with fresh fish that he kept in a red plastic bucket. "Come see!" he said. We waved him off. "No!" he insisted. "Come see fish!" We explained that we were going surfing and did not need any fish. "Beautiful fish!" he said. Rick peered into the bucket and agreed; it was a beautiful fish. We *did* have the facilities to cook, and it didn't look like we could ignore Mohammed for the whole week.

"How about tomorrow?" Rick asked.

"Tomorrow?" Mohammed repeated, his bushy eyebrows raised. "Tomorrow fish?"

Rick agreed.

"Yes," Mohammed said, nodding vigorously. "Tomorrow fish!" He waved at us, his thick, black mustache curved upward with his wide smile as we drove off.

We checked every point and bay on the way north, figuring we'd end up surfing Tamri again. I'd heard about a lively souk, or market, a few hundred kilometers north. We'd planned to drive there later in the week but when we arrived at Tamri—where solid close-outs were breaking far outside, offering nothing to ride—we decided to keep driving north to Essaouira. We had longboards on the roof and little cash, but our gas tank was full and our curiosity piqued.

The countryside whirled by in a blur, the road intersecting fertile valleys then winding up and over barren hillsides, the Berlingo buffeted by strong winds as we summited high ridges. Several times the strong gusts readjusted the longboards and we were forced to stop. The drive stretched on.

Finally we pulled just short of the entrance to what we hoped was the souk and paid a man a few dirhams to park on the street. We had no choice but to hope the longboards would remain unmolested in our absence.

As we neared the heart of the souk the shaded streets became crowded with pedestrians and the mood turned from hushed to lively in a matter of blocks: a man in a hooded, maroon robe pushed a rickety wooden cart piled high with fresh mint; bearded men sold olives out of large plastic drums; women covered head-to-toe in layers of satiny fabric carried shopping bags full of tangerines, baguettes, and freshly killed chickens. The maze of streets seemed endless. Side corridors stacked with red and blue milk crates led into darkness while the main artery was packed with locals: pairs of women in headscarves, groups of men in grubby sweatshirts and cheap plastic sandals, old ladies with shrunken mouths, all of them shopping and going about their day. Clothing shops sold the long robes favored by the women next to skimpy bikinis imported from China; tiny spice shops offered little tiered tables with conical piles of powdered curry and paprika, plastic tubs of various roots (some labeled as Viagra), or chunks of fragrant musk. Inside, brightly colored rows of pottery lined shelves that extended to the ceiling. I nodded at the few other tourists but didn't stop to chat, tempting as it was to share my sense of enchantment.

Occasionally, a shop owner standing outside gave us a pleasant nod and an invitation to "Come see." (I was beginning to wonder if "Come see" was the country's slogan: Morocco, the Come See! State.) But we pressed on, overwhelmed and intoxicated by the new sights, smells, and constant activity. Every corner held more surprises: a cage packed with choose-your-own chickens; a hooded specter of a man silently smoking tobacco next to a pair of nervous, flightless roosters; a cart piled high with bright tangerines; a narrow alley lined with various sizes (some several feet tall) of curvy, fabric-and-metal lamps in rich shades of red and orange.

But only the shopkeepers hoping to reel us in made eye contact. Nobody wanted their picture taken, or, it seemed, to be noticed by us. I'd read about this sensitivity and heard about it from my aunt, who had traveled to Morocco a few years back. She told me to be especially careful of photographing the women and to ask first of anyone else. But I couldn't help myself—this souk was like a new planet—my finger remained glued to the shutter. I tried to be discreet. I tried being sneaky. But at a food stall, where a pair of aproned women cooked square, doughy pancakes on a hot black griddle as fast as passersby could purchase them, I got caught.

Rick and Kurt were buying one pancake each, smeared with thick honey, and I couldn't resist trying to capture the scene, even though from inside the stall's narrow, dimly lit restaurant a few customers had begun to glare at us. Just after I snuck a photo of the women, a young man brushed hard past my shoulder, growling,

"Why you take picture." I turned to him, my mouth agape, my mind trying to spin a satisfactory response—some way to explain my embarrassing curiosity. But the man was not looking for an answer; the milling crowd swallowed him before I could utter, "So I will remember."

Finally we gave in to one of the beckoning shopkeepers and stepped into one of the spice shops. The jolly host introduced himself as Mohammed and made us comfortable on silky floor pillows. A few moments later as the four of us made small talk, a weathered man entered with a pot of tea and three mismatched glass cups. Mohammed dismissed him with a slight nod and poured for us.

I gave in to the knowledge that this hospitality would come at a price and sure enough, when our tea cups ran dry, Mohammed began seducing us with spices. From various glass jars lining the walls, he pulled cinnamon, coriander, saffron, depositing them each in a fine mesh square of fabric that he twisted closed to create a tiny ball that he then placed in front of our noses for us to "sample." He educated us on each spice's origin and its uses. When Mohammed noticed Rick's leaky sinuses (from our surf the day before) he jumped on the opportunity, suavely combining spices and powders in a mesh bag, then holding it to Rick's nose.

"For the cold," Mohammed said.

Rick waved him off. "It's not a cold," he said, motioning riding a wave with his hand.

"Ah," Mohammed said, not missing a beat. "This good for that, too." He placed the mesh bag right beneath Rick's left nostril and modeled a big sniff.

Unable to escape, Rick inhaled but immediately began coughing and snorting. "Ohmygod!" he cried between rubs of his nose. "What the hell'd you put in there? Fire powder?" Mohammed just chuckled. Rick's nasal passages would continue to burn for days to come.

Because of our promise to Mr. Tomorrow Fish, Rick bought a small mixture of a fish-compatible spice. I haggled for a pair of hand-painted pottery bowls. As a parting gift, Mohammed gave me a chunk of soft yellow jasmine, which I still have in the depths of my linen closet. When I snap fresh sheets onto the bed, a reminder of the fragrant and captivating souk returns.

———————|———————

On the ride home from Essaouira we decided to capitalize on the early incoming tide the next morning with a crack-of-dawn start. When Kurt's watch alarm went off in the darkness, we got up, made coffee, carried our boards up the tight stairs, loaded up, and headed north. We stopped at Boilers Point where a sandstone slab with deep crisscrossed grooves guarded the shore. Huge waves thundered forth in the blackness, one after the other, curtains of mist illuminated by the moonlight. With the ground shaking from the collapsing waves, we knew it wasn't worth the wait for dawn. We checked every point on the way south, with the same result. The big swell had arrived indeed, but there was no place to ride it.

After checking several bays and points, the skies were still dark. I checked my watch and cursed.

"What?" Kurt asked.

"Know what time it is?" I grumbled.

"Oops," Kurt said, sheepish. We'd gotten up at 4:30, not 5:30 as we'd agreed.

"You're fired from alarm duty," I said.

As the sun began its rise over the desert, we pulled into a dirt lot closest to Anchor Point, the best-known break in the area for its extra-long rides and regularity, and found the crowds. With visions of Ollies Point dancing in my head, I'd hoped to get a crack at Anchor's, but as we scampered out to the mini rock peninsula my anticipation fizzled. At least thirty shortboarders, with a constant stream of more jumping off the rocky access point, dominated the lineup. Rifling, deep-blue waves framed by the rock-slab shore peeled the entire length of the bay. A few feet overhead, more on the sets. Steep and hollow and gorgeous. But not for longboarders. I watched a shortboarder fight his way into a wave, slice low into the trough, then back up, sending spray over the lip before soaring down again. Up and down he went, over and over until I lost sight of him as his wave continued on toward the distant beach.

The three of us sat while the rising sun illuminated the diamond-glitter spray from the waves and cast an orange glow across the rocks. Local women wearing head scarves and layered, full-length dresses soaked to the knees with saltwater hacked mussels off the rocks in the low, low tide, oblivious to the flocks of surfers swirling around them.

———————

For some unknown reason, Bananas had a bad rap—some called it mushy, others claimed it was jam-packed with kooks and beginners—but maybe those who'd spread such rumors had never surfed it on a twelve-foot swell. The paddle-out was straightforward, in a channel along the rocky cliff's edge. The wave was a nice, rolling peeler, and the beginners stayed on the far inside and mostly out of the way. My only complaint was the crowds. Because the swell was so big, surfers were concentrated at Bananas and Anchor Point.

We set up shop at Bananas. When a newcomer paddled into the lineup to try to shake up the order we had going, Kurt or Rick would out-paddle them or I'd pick off a set wave and things would be right again. The rides were long—not as long as Ollies but still fun, and the offshores groomed the peaks to perfect shape. The cool water required a full spring-weight wetsuit but without accessories, so I was able to feel the bumpy wax surface of my Drifter under the pads of my feet as well as the ocean bathing my toes. It was a nice little setup at Bananas, and we made full use of it each morning. Afternoons were ridiculously crowded, so we sometimes talked each other into surfing Alligator Rock, a sandy point a few kilometers north that offered speedy, wind-blown close-outs, and ended up enjoying it for the goofing off and the chance to rinse off the dust. Some afternoons we didn't surf at all, instead hanging out at La Bas drinking café au laits or mint tea, getting Moroccan cooking lessons from Rachid, reading or napping back at the apartment, or playing with Omar, a cuddly stray cat who had adopted us.

---

On our second to last day, we exited the Berlingo and stepped to the edge of the dusty cliff overlooking the takeoff at Bananas, shivering in the crisp desert darkness, the sky above still twinkling with fading stars. The waves below echoed their feathery whisper as they swept the walls of the cliff. It sounded big, but it always does in the near-dark, so I didn't pay it much mind. We dressed as usual, grabbed our boards, and padded in bare feet down the rocky trail along the cliff to the sand.

There were two factors at play that made that particular morning doomed to disaster: the tidal zone at Bananas is composed of sharp, low-lying rocks and deep sand "holes"—both impossible to see in the dark; and such a big swell coupled with a full-moon, rapidly flooding tide created a dangerously powerful current.

I picked my way as best I could through the rocks at the water's edge, bracing myself and trying to stay balanced as spent waves flooded by, inching closer to deeper water so I could hop on my board during a lull and paddle like hell. But there was no lull. Massive, blue black boomers expelled themselves in long, tunneling walls; through the darkness I could just make out the white spray shearing from the lips by the steady offshore wind. The noise of it all, the constant thundering of wave after wave after wave plus the thick shorebreak pulsing forward and washing back crowded into my ears, making it difficult to think.

I inched forward, got blasted, inched forward, braced myself, inched forward, jammed my toes on the sharp, barnacled rocks, waded a step or two farther, stumbled into a hole, steadied myself, shuffled forward, braced myself, watched for a lull, thought I had one, and hopped on. The booming and the wind blared in my ears and blended with my breath as I stroked with deep, committed strokes. I kept an eye on the side of the cliff to mark my progress but it seemed as if I was going nowhere. I dug harder.

I could just see Rick scratching over a wave. *Wow*, I thought, *it is big*—Rick was still paddling up. *But he's doing it*, I thought, *so I can too*. I wondered why the channel, normally like a conveyer belt, didn't seem to be working. The side of the cliff began to drift away as I was picked up by the powerful side-shore current. And yet I paddled harder, my arms working in synch with my breathing as I made it over pile after pile of whitewash until I came face to face with a set wave, poised to break. I turtled my board beneath it, flipped upright, and started paddling again.

Another wave, another turtle, stroke, stroke, stroke . . . another wave, got smashed and lost my board, yanked on the leash as the next wave loomed, hurried onto the board, paddled, paddled, fought over the whitewash, stroked, breathed, stroked, took a big breath, held it, turtled, flipped, paddled . . . turtled, flipped, mounted the board, another wave upon me, up the face, no, no, no, don't break! Backward over the falls, slammed, pinned down, up for air, where's my board? Yanked the leash, slid on, paddled, turtled, the board's rail hitting me in the head, inhaled seawater, surfaced, got on the board, panicked now, where's Kurt? Where's Rick? Turtled, flipped, coughed, arms ached with fatigue. Next one was scary-big, paddled with arms on fire, the wave broke, I tried to punch through the lip but got ripped upward and slammed down and my mind hit full-tilt panic, *get me the hell outta here.*

I swam deep beneath the next wave then reeled in my board and paddled hard toward shore with booming waves exploding everywhere. I kept an eye behind me for unbroken waves, afraid to ditch my board in case the leash snapped, marooning me in the impact zone against the strong current. Bear-hugging my board, I rode a turbulent wall of white water into the shallows, my breath shaky in my chest. I stepped gingerly onto the rocks, the razor-sharp barnacles cutting into my feet.

The whitewash pulsed all around me, knocking me off balance. I stumbled, falling into the bed of rocks, picked myself and my board up—forgetting to worry about dings or scratches in the fiberglass—and stepped forward, the board as heavy as a red-wood, my arm aching, my mind blank. More white water, more stumbling. My whole body shivered, my eyes down, squinting in the faint moonlight for a way over a surface like shattered glass, my tender feet burning, the wide band of soft, feathery sand still a mile away. The tears began to fall even as I tried to hold them back. *Concentrate: one foot down, shift weight slowly, breathe.* I braced as water pushed by me, putting the next foot down, shifting my weight, stumbling, shaking.

I looked up and saw Kurt walking toward me in the dawn light, picking his way across the rocks. He and Rick had given up too. Still I moved forward . . . *I can do this, damnit!*

"You OK?" he said to me.

"Uh-huh," I said, wobbling, tears blurring my vision.

"Let me take your board," he said.

"I got it," I blubbered.

"Here," he said gently, removing the board from my grip, the sudden release of its weight improving my balance but compounding my sense of failure. When I reached the soft sand, I sat down and cried. Then, hand-in-hand, Kurt and I turned our backs on the waves and left. Later that morning, we surfed big, fluffy waves in the large bay just south of town, but the experience at Bananas still haunted me and my heart wasn't in it. I soon paddled in while Kurt and Rick rallied, claiming their best waves of the trip.

———————

A week after returning home to Sicily, Kurt developed a strange rash on his chest. I, too, wasn't feeling right, as if that day at Bananas had permanently upset my equilibrium. I wondered if Kurt and I had been poisoned somehow, maybe picked up a rare parasite or infection from the barnacles cutting our feet. After running some tests they called us to come in for the results. The receptionist refused to offer specifics, which I took as a very bad sign.

Kurt and I waited inside the little room, out of our minds with worry. Did we have Ebola? Mercury poisoning from Mr. Tomorrow Fish's daily catch? Radiation sickness?

The doctor, a friend of ours named Kris, entered and sat. He pulled a small tube of something from his lab coat pocket and handed it to Kurt.

"What's this?" Kurt asked.

"It's for your ringworm," Kris said, smirking.

"Huh?"

"You've got ringworm."

Kurt looked at me and at the same moment we uttered, "Omar!" Kurt had often cuddled with the stray—Omar had become so accustomed to his attention that one day when we hadn't returned for our afternoon nap, he revenge-peed all over our bed.

Kris turned to me, one of his eyebrows raised.

"What?" I asked anxiously.

Kris grinned. "You're pregnant."

My stomach did a flip and my heart pounded. Kurt and I had been trying to become parents for several years with no luck.

"Are you sure?" I breathed.

"I'm sure," Kris said.

Kurt grabbed me and together we danced around the room.

Approximately nine months later, on September 17, 2007, at 7:04 in the evening, Elsa Lynn Waeschle officially joined Team Creep.

# 11

## AND BABY MAKES THREE

SOMETIME AFTER MIDNIGHT I woke to swirling orange lights washing eerily over the dunes. Alarmed, I sat up in our rented caravan's tiny bed, wondering if we were about to be booted by the beach police. After driving a long and dusty road, we'd settled in for the night at the edge of a sandy cliff, the restless Atlantic beyond darkening beneath dusky skies. We hadn't seen any signs indicating that we couldn't catch a few winks, but maybe Portugal had unwritten rules about parking your caravan any- where you pleased. I cringed at the thought of having to wake Elsa; I wondered where we would go.

"It's just the trash truck," Kurt mumbled after taking a peek out the windows.

"All the way out here?" I asked. We'd been impressed by Portugal's spotless beaches, each with rubbish and recycling kiosks staked out every 100 meters and a staff of employees who walked the tide line each morning to collect what the ocean deposited overnight.

"I guess they take this trash thing pretty seriously," Kurt replied, wiggling back under the covers.

I thought of Sicily's trash-lined shores and wondered what the

beaches would look like if people took care of them. I spooned up
to Kurt and closed my eyes.

———————|———————

In between checking beaches for surf, we'd spent the last few
days weaving through eucalyptus groves and black-barked pine
forests, enjoying the clean, fresh coastal air. We explored tiny
whitewashed villages with red-tile roofs clinging to sunny hillsides, passed rows of young corn planted in uneven rows and
wildflower gardens bursting with color. Elsa, who would smoke a
contest for World's Easiest Baby, would fall asleep as per her usual any-
time attached to a vibrating chassis or coo at passersby as we strolled
the open-air markets. We were completely charmed by Portugal's
wild stretches of untrammeled hillsides and cobblestone streets, by
the handmade farmers cheeses and the colorful ceramics, and the
people living simple, hearty lives without cell phones or even cars.
But we'd come for the waves, and it seemed that there weren't any.

Our expectations were low, however—it's not like Portugal
is known for its summer surf. And because of Kurt's ridiculously
busy work schedule for the months leading up to the trip, we felt
like strangers, so we had decided to make this trip more about
exploring a new place as a family than scoring epic surf.

Secretly, though, I was desperate for waves. My pregnancy
had been more like a nine-month stint with food poisoning, and
since Elsa's birth I'd surfed exactly twice, both times the waves
inconsistent and small. I'd exhausted myself just paddling for
them. Recently I had been in Ventura, California, for a short work
contract, but the closest I got to the fun waves breaking at C-Street
was watching other surfers ride them from my hotel room while I
pumped breast milk. It was the first time I'd been away from Elsa
and I don't know what depressed me more—not starting my day
with her in my arms or the fact that a place existed where people

could surf every day and I didn't live there.

I needed waves. I needed to know that after a year-and-a-half hiatus, after childbirth and breastfeeding and the demands of motherhood, that the magic of riding waves still lived in me.

———————+———————

Just outside of the known surfer's stronghold of Carrapateira, we finally encountered the promising sight of car roof racks with surfboards. We followed a dusty but well-kept dirt road toward a beach called Praia Amado and stopped at the edge of a bluff sloping down to honey-colored sands. Packed with dusty caravans and cars from all over Europe, the parking lot felt like the fairgrounds of a Grateful Dead show complete with skinny dogs asleep in the dirt and faded laundry flapping in the wind.

A peek over the cliff revealed moderate-sized but scruffy waves breaking inside a semi-protected bay. A dozen or so shortboarders hovered in a lineup just below us while one longboarder floated alone in the wind-blown swells far to the south. Kurt and I looked at each other and shrugged.

Elsa rode on Kurt's shoulders as we walked the length of the beach to stretch our legs and better assess the conditions. After passing the pack of shortboarders riding the wind-chop, we passed surf camp after surf camp, the formula the same: one instructor stood in front of a logoed flag in ankle-deep water watching a dozen learners run over each other in the whitewash, their arms flopping wildly, their hoots and hollers lost to the relentless wind and pounding surf. Fifty yards later, in front of a different flag, another group would be doing the same thing. One instructor stood talking into his cell phone and facing away from his charges, which made me worry— surfing can be dangerous, what if one of them got hurt?

Meanwhile, the farther we distanced ourselves from the parking lot, the less clothed people became until suddenly, there were naked people everywhere. At the far end of the beach, we even passed a deeply tanned, long-haired man with no tan lines sitting cross-legged in the sand. No tan lines. It took effort not to look a second time.

We quickly returned to the parking lot and Kurt surfed first, taking out the 6'4" shortboard we'd purchased the winter before to better ride Sicily's short-fetch wind chop. Praia Amado would be its maiden voyage and Kurt's first time on a shortboard since college. My time with Elsa passed quickly—she was hungry, wanted to practice walking, and then needed a nap. Kurt returned a while later, grinning with stoke.

Because the longboard was currently being used as part of Elsa's makeshift crib, I decided to try the 6'4". As I walked barefoot across the pebbly dirt parking lot down to below the tide line where the saturated sand was hard and dense, I realized how alone I felt without Kurt: attaching his leash next to me, paddling out in front of me, and sitting nearby in the lineup, cracking jokes or elbowing his way into a crowd.

The water at first felt bracingly cold, the steady wind an unfriendly presence against my cheek. I stuck close to a large rock, sitting just left of it in the hopes of having a corner of the surf to myself. But the tide had changed and an experienced crowd had moved in, dominating the lineup. I came in shivering as the sun dipped behind a cottony haze, without catching one wave. Meanwhile, Kurt had brought Elsa down to wait for me and couldn't wait to leave.

"I was surrounded by boobs," he whimpered. Neutral on the whole topless thing, he had been boxed in. "I had four British girls simultaneously applying sunscreen to their breasts like they were the Karate Kid waxing cars. This other woman peeled off her wetsuit right in front of me and she had no top on underneath! In the middle of all that, a woman was totally covered up trying to breastfeed in this tent back along the cliff. It was so weird."

Blame it on the boobs, but before leaving the beach Kurt had somehow forgotten to completely fasten Elsa's stroller straps and the minute we hit the rocky dirt path she tumbled right out, splatting head-first. I saw it all in slow-motion: Elsa leaning forward, probably to play with the strap the way she always does, but this time she kept going, folding forward, landing face-down in the dirt. I stood stunned in my dripping wetsuit as Kurt scooped her up, her little body still in shock. Then the long pause before a heaving wail, tears, and sobs. Spectators gave us a wide berth as Kurt consoled Elsa, a bright red but superficial scratch on her forehead. Soon she was smiling again, such is her nature, but Kurt and I felt like we should be publicly flogged.

That night, strong gusts buffeted our little camper, which we'd parked on the dry, shrubby plain overlooking Amado's rocky coast. I lay awake, wondering why I hadn't tried to take a wave that afternoon. What was I so afraid of? The shallow bottom? The rocks? Failure? Would I spend the whole trip chasing waves in anguish?

When by 7:00 AM, Elsa still hadn't made a peep, I immediately concluded that the previous day's tumble had given her a head injury and she was in a coma. Kurt and I are both EMTs, which gives us just enough knowledge to make us paranoid. But Kurt found Elsa awake, playing quietly.

"How many fingers am I holding up?" Kurt asked her.

Elsa gave him her morning-star smile and cooed, kicking her feet.

Kurt scooped her up and the three of us cuddled in bed for fifteen precious minutes before I rolled out to make coffee and check the surf.

---

Hoping for better conditions, we continued our way south, stopping at hidden coves, wide, sandy beaches, and rocky points—all pristine and spotless and framed by lovely green blue, sapphire, or cobalt seas, but with no surf. We ended up drinking *café com leites* in a courtyard paved with pale, hand-hewn cobbles in Sagres, a town set high on sea-carved cliffs, a stone's throw from Africa.

"Should we wait it out?" I asked Kurt. A local surf shop owner had just told us it had been flat for days.

"Maybe we should check that beach, what was it called?" We'd met a group of caravanning Germans who'd told us of a beach nicely protected from the wind. "Monte Clerigo."

Kurt tore off another piece of croissant and fed it to Elsa, who smacked her lips and hummed. "We've gotta work our way back up north anyways . . . "

"We might as well start now," I finished.

After a detour to the urban confusion of Lagosh for groceries, we turned the camper north. On a whim we drove the long, sinuous, and scary dirt track down to Praia da Cordoama, site of a recent surf competition. The aquamarine waves looked relatively mild, so I took out the longboard while Kurt sat in the shade on the hot beach trying to keep cool and keep Elsa entertained. I caught a few waves, but other than my joy of reuniting with the Drifter, the session was mostly forgettable: windy, choppy, inconsistent. Apparently it was worse than I thought because when I showed up at the camper to give Kurt his turn, he passed.

"North?" Kurt asked as he negotiated the camper out of the crowded parking lot.

"North," I replied.

————————|————————

As we rounded the last bend after a long drive, both of us inhaled in surprise. "We finally found it, Amy," Kurt said as we pulled to a stop above Monte Clerigo, grinning. "It only took us three days but we found it."

The fading daylight cast a warm glow across a sheltered, sandy beach separated into two halves by a large mound of rocks. Below, a group of half a dozen longboarders sat in a lineup of clean and glassy midsized waves, a slick gunmetal gray beneath a lowering sun. Fun waves. Not windy. Not crowded.

And the camping was dreamy. A few kilometers past the beach, a neat gravel road high above the water offered fenced pull-outs perfect for the rig, perched at the edge of cliffs layered with red and black bands of rock, with sweeping coastal views. We chose the first with flat ground and called it home. Breaking waves along the beach below and gentle winds formed the perfect background to our evening, cooking Bavarian sausage and fresh broccoli on our little stove and rocking an overtired Elsa to sleep.

Looking back, one of us (Kurt, actually, as it was his turn) should have surfed that night. It's a lesson I have learned many times, maybe this time it will finally stick: the surf you see in any given moment is just that, a moment. It won't last. It may not be there in the morning. If you see good surf, you forget your plans, your needs (you may even need to put aside your family's), and you surf. Not in an hour, or in the morning, but right then.

But we didn't surf that night, and in the morning the wave was tiny, with funky currents on the inside. Nothing to ride. Disappointed, we checked the other two beaches nearby but came up empty.

We decided to wait it out at Monte Clerigo for a few days. After sampling some decent chest-high surf on the 6'4" that afternoon, Kurt came in to give me a turn when a thick fog rolled in, making the waves invisible. We waited again, hoping for conditions to improve, but the fog's wispy tendrils seemed to engulf us further. By five o'clock I decided we might all benefit from an early night. We could extend the camper's awning, sit outside and enjoy the evening with some *vinho verde* and cold roasted chicken that we'd bought at the Lagosh supermarket. But Elsa was so tired I had to practically arm-wrestle her to sleep. Then the fog lifted. As I collapsed into bed shortly before sunset, I imagined the long, fun waves surely breaking. From our campsite high on the cliff, I could hear their soft crush against the rocks and beach, pulling at me like a drug.

We woke to more fog the next morning and stalled for time by taking a long walk below the tide line, our bare feet chilled by the hard, wet sand and Elsa content on Kurt's shoulders. No other footprints mixed with our own and the dusky haze shrouded the tiny village, the road, even the lifeguard towers. We reminisced about our life in Sicily, which would be ending soon. We were ready to return to our families and to doing the things we loved: surfing the Straights and Short Sands, mountain biking, making our favorite raspberry-honey jam, hosting summer barbeques in our grassy backyard.

Later that morning I paddled out on the 6'4" to surf empty waves cloaked in the soupy fog. I enjoyed figuring out the squirrelly little board, despite falling off the back of it once and banging my temple against the rails during a wipeout. That afternoon, after walking the cobblestone streets of Aljezura, the nearby town, we returned to the beach so Kurt could catch the evening glass-off. The next morning I paddled out for one more session, this time on the longboard, before we pulled stakes. I caught a few waves but the tide was lowering quickly, making the fickle peaks break closer to shore and in rapidly shallowing water. My old confidence and comfort with surfing still felt a ways off, and we'd decided to try for better luck up north. I hoped it would pay off. From surfing bloomed a quiet sense of contentment and inner peace that I ached to reconnect with before it disappeared completely.

———————————————

After six hours of driving, through busy and congested Lisbon and the industrial wastelands in its wake, we began scouring the coast for surf. But the only people riding the massive, windblown swells were kiteboarders launching huge airs and zipping along the frothy surface. With our options dwindling and daylight fading, we managed to find a cliffside overlook near an unfinished housing development and settled in for the night. It was a far cry from our tranquil spot above Monte Clerigo, but it would have to do.

In the morning we continued our search and had all but given up when the coastline changed. The wide, exposed beaches transitioned to private, protected coves and broad points catching neat lines of swell. We watched a near-perfect wave peeling off of a rock-slab point at Praia de Sao Lourenco, a deserted beach with not a single car in the parking lot. At every beach, waves were breaking, unmolested, all over the place. It was eight o'clock. Where was everybody?

Finally, at a distant, dagger-shaped point with big walls of surging swell breaking, we saw surfers—all six of them. "If this was Southern California there'd be fifty people in the water already," Kurt said as we assessed a beach called Ribeira d'Ilhas from a wooden platform halfway up the side of the cliff.

Incredibly, Ilhas offered not one but three distinct waves: a far-off point peeling with groomed, consistent walls, a mushy middle-ground wave breaking over rock-slab shoals, and another pseudo point breaking in front of a narrow wedge of sandy beach. "I'm getting in," Kurt said, hurrying back to the camper. About that time the tide began its flood into the bay, and with it came the crowds.

It started as a trickle, a car here, a caravan there, a scruffy youth walking out for a closer look at the waves, then gearing up and paddling out. Then a surf camp van arrived with a trailer full of boards, dumping a dozen kids onto the beach. Then came the families—dads toting longboards and the beach umbrella for mom and the little ones, then came the pack of local kids—some of them wearing team Billabong wetsuits and their boards splattered with stickers advertising sponsors like Roxy and Red Bull—girls and boys who, as Kurt put it after surfing alongside them, "at seventeen are already better surfers than I'll *ever* be."

I was excited to surf but because of the crowds I didn't mind waiting. As a special treat, I watched Kurt surf, something that's difficult to do from the lineup. On a shortboard, Kurt's style is not so much the modern thrash and burn, but a smooth and easy grace that reminded me of a snowboarder carving broad turns down a virgin-powdered slope. I grinned as I watched him catch his last few waves, the joy I sensed in him filling me up.

At high tide, with the crowds thinning, I stood on the shore with the Drifter under my arm as the thick shorepound washed up the steep sands, and felt, well, nervous. I had tried to be low-key about catching good waves on this trip. If Portugal didn't produce, surely our old haunts would after we moved home to the Northwest in a little less than a year. But looking at the nice waves with so few surfers to compete against, I could sense my expectations growing.

Because of the pointlike setup, the paddle-out was easy and I reached the lineup with dry hair. It always takes me a little while to get a feel for a new place, so I watched a few others take waves until my desires got the better of me. I turned and paddled and missed my first wave, then my second. I sat, watching again, trying to relax and get in tune with the ocean. I boldly paddled for a set wave and missed. Finally I caught a wave but a shortboarder caught it, too, inside of me, which is sort of bad manners on his part, but after I'd missed so many waves I suppose I couldn't blame him. I popped up anyway, feeling sluggish and slow to my feet. With nowhere to go, I straightened out as the wave folded behind me and the shortboarder continued on, zipping up and down the face. I steered over the whitewash, then paddled back out, dejected. Was I going to have to learn to do this all over again?

I decided to take a risk and relocate deeper. Suddenly a wave rose up from the middle section and headed *right for me*, and before I knew it I was paddling with two easy strokes and was on my feet, gliding down the face of a smooth wall, past the shortboarder who'd dropped in on me earlier. I carved low to slow my pace, then skimmed high toward the crest to catch up with the speed-section that had re-formed on the inside. I rode that burst of energy toward the beach, unwilling to relinquish a single second of that sweet reunion. The joy of the moment was the spark I needed.

So I did it again. And again. Each time trusting my instincts and the mystery of the experience. I couldn't figure out why I was still alone at my deeper takeoff. I was catching a lot of waves. So many, in fact, that I started feeling guilty. About that time I noticed that the sun seemed a little lower, but on this trip, Kurt's first words when I returned from the waves had always been, "Why didn't you stay out longer?"

So I caught more waves, each ride puffing a little bit more wind back into my sails.

The sun was starting to look a lot lower then, and I had just taken a pretty good beating from an outside set that had caught me inside during one of my paddle-outs. It seemed like a good time to head for shore, but it took me awhile because just then my calf muscle seized into the worst leg cramp I've ever had. Once I recovered, I almost dropped in on an exposed rock. Finally, exhausted and spooked, I belly-rode a little inside wave to the beach and practically crawled on hands and knees out of the surf. My biceps and lower back ached, my lips and hairline felt fried, my spasming calf gave me a limp. But behind that, my connection to the waves had been restored. I was elated, and couldn't wait to share it with Kurt.

But when I approached the camper, Elsa was crying. With my mama anxiety meter pegged, I quickly put down my board and stripped off my wetsuit, discarding it into the dirt. Elsa hardly ever cries—as a newborn we nearly starved her to death because she didn't let us know she was hungry.

"You're finally back," Kurt said as I peeked inside. He was slumped in the passenger seat holding Elsa, her eyes red and tears wetting her cheeks.

"What's wrong?" I asked, wrapping a towel around my waist and plucking Elsa from Kurt's lap. She immediately stopped crying and hung her arms around my neck. Her warm baby smell hit me like a freight train and I hugged her tight.

"You were just gone for so long," Kurt moaned. "Like five hours."

I peered at the clock on the dash. I'd been gone exactly three and a half and casually told him so. Elsa smiled at me and started pulling at my wet hair.

"Oh," Kurt said. "Well it felt like five."

"I think maybe the daddy clock ticks a little slower," I said in an effort to diffuse his agitation. Kurt scrubbed his face with his hands and disappeared into the back of the camper. I took Elsa for a stroll to give Kurt some time to recoup. I knew he was thinking about all the long shifts he'd been working lately and the days when he went cycling with friends while I was sweating in the heat at home, pureeing baby food and doing laundry. I knew he realized that a three-and-a-half hour surf session was a pretty meager payback for all the waves I'd missed since moving to Sicily. But I also knew that I'd left him hanging, and that I didn't want to hear Elsa cry like that again.

"Did you catch some good waves, at least?" Kurt asked later that night. We had secured a flat spot above San Lourenço, the orange sun setting while we washed down yet another cold roasted chicken with Super Bocks and Elsa played in her makeshift crib.

I told him I had. I told him about sitting deep, about the first wave I caught and the ease with which I'd scored those after it. I told him about how it felt strangely satisfying to get caught inside by that set wave, going over the falls backward, my leash tangling around my ankles for a scary instant. I told him about an inspiring stand-up surfer I'd seen stroke into a wave from way outside using his long paddle and ride it all the way to the beach, about the perfectly peeling waves I rode far into the inside, about belly-riding my last wave in because I was too worn out to stand.

"I wanted so badly to be out there with you," Kurt said, stroking Elsa's downy head. "It's just not as much fun alone, is it?"

"No," I said. "It really isn't." I wondered, though. The elation I'd felt was real, but was it less fun without him or just a different, more private kind of fun? I tried to picture myself on an entire surf trip without Kurt, but it was impossible. I realized that sharing my experiences with the person I love, whether we were trading waves or just watching each other from the beach, made it complete. I sat back as the sun slipped into the blackening sea. "Someday we'll all be out there together," I added.

"Yes," Kurt replied, scooping up Elsa, who hugged him back. "I can't wait."

# ACKNOWLEDGMENTS

I WOULD LIKE TO THANK Kate Rogers, Janet Kimball, Shanna Knowlton, and the excellent staff at The Mountaineers Books for their thoughtful guidance and support. Many thanks to Julie Van Pelt for her keen eye and insightful review and to Colin Chisholm for his help with the details. To Kasey Kersnowski, Cheryl Endo, Carin Knutson, and the editing staff at Patagonia for their friendship and support of my writing and this book. Thanks also to Sarah Wallace, Marcus Sanders, Bryan Dickerson, and Anne Beasley: editors who made a difference.

Special thanks also to Benedetta Leanza, *la migliore bambinaia*; Denny Shelton for Portgual; Jeff Abandonato at Cheka-Looka Surf Shop for his kindness; Leah Kiviat for her friendship; Clem Smith, Chip McKeever, and Jason Peck for their acceptance and push in the right direction; Jenny Stewart and the Surf Sisters (especially Karen); Shani Cranston of Milagro Retreats; Joe and Holly Walsh and the many friends at Witch's Rock Surf Camp.

I would like to thank my family for their support, especially my mother for her enthusiasm and my dad for believing in me. To Rick Ratcliff for his WAP enabling and for enhancing every go-out, and to Kitty, for being way more than a Voice of Reason.

But most of all, I would like to thank Kurt, for being my best friend, and Mother Ocean, whose waves keep me wandering.

THE MOUNTAINEERS, founded in 1906, is a nonprofit outdoor activity and conservation club, whose mission is "to explore, study, preserve, and enjoy the natural beauty of the outdoors. . . . " Based in Seattle, Washington, the club is now one of the largest such organizations in the United States, with seven branches throughout Washington State.

The Mountaineers sponsors both classes and year-round outdoor activities in the Pacific Northwest, which include hiking, mountain climbing, ski-touring, snowshoeing, bicycling, camping, canoeing and kayaking, nature study, sailing, and adventure travel. The club's conservation division supports environmental causes through educational activities, sponsoring legislation, and presenting informational programs. All club activities are led by skilled, experienced volunteers, who are dedicated to promoting safe and responsible enjoyment and preservation of the outdoors.

If you would like to participate in these organized outdoor activities or the club's programs, consider a membership in The Mountaineers. For information and an application, write or call The Mountaineers, Club Headquarters, 7700 Sand Point Way NE, Seattle, WA 98115; 206-521-6001. You can also visit the club's website at www.mountaineers.org or contact The Mountaineers via email at clubmail@mountaineers.org.

The Mountaineers Books, an active, nonprofit publishing program of the club, produces guidebooks, instructional texts, historical works, natural history guides, and works on environmental conservation. All books produced by The Mountaineers Books fulfill the club's mission.

*Send or call for our catalog of more than 450 outdoor titles:*

 The Mountaineers Books
1001 SW Klickitat Way, Suite 201
Seattle, WA 98134
800-553-4453
mbooks@mountaineersbooks.org
www.mountaineersbooks.org